MY 92 YEARS
ON SANIBEL

Remembering My Family And My Island

by Francis Bailey

as told to Emilie Alfino

This book is dedicated to
my parents, Frank Bailey and Annie Mead Matthews Bailey;
my grandmother Hallie Matthews, known to all as Granny;
and my Aunt Charlotta, affectionately called "Chebum";
as well as to all of the people, too numerous to name,
who have affected my life in so many wonderful ways.

Author's Note
This is a memoir, and the people and events
described herein, including times I may quote
someone, are to the best of my memory.
Any mistakes are my own.

Additional Help
was provided by Renny Severance, former
editor of the Island Reporter and The Islander,
in the design and layout of this book and processing
photographs to bring out the best in them for printing.

Contents

INTRODUCTION

At one time I thought I was something of a writer, and I have been thinking about this book since 1948 but took little or no action. I think the word "procrastination" was coined for me. But life got busy. Now I'm 91, my brothers Sam and John are gone, and my health is not what it used to be, to say the least.

How fast time goes! When you're 20, five years is a quarter of your life; when you're 80, it's one sixteenth – yet it's the same amount of time.

I wanted to put down on paper some things that my children may not know or did not pay attention to when I told them. That's no slam – I did the same thing when I was young – and then later you wish you had paid more attention or asked more questions.

I talked about writing – not novels, but this type of stuff, or stories. This would be in the spring of 1936. I wrote a little history of the island as I remember it. In prep school we wrote a theme nearly every week. Our English teacher would give us titles, and we would pick one and write. In college, I spent some time in the library but often I would just start writing, sometimes until 7 a.m., shower and just go to class. I won some nice books for the stories I wrote in school. One was about ships and I forget what the other one was about. I won two books as a prize for this one:

By Francis Bailey at 15 years old
Essay for Eng. II (Spring 1936, freshman, prep school)

Sanibel

Situated midway between Tampa and Key West, Florida, is a small island known as Sanibel which is a Spanish word for the beautiful island of Isabella. On this island Gasparilla was supposed to have buried all his riches. Many men have spent years hunting for it but so far none has been found and most people take it as a legend. On its sister island, called Captiva, Gasperilla kept his captives. This is a known fact.

The first settlements of this island were made about 1814 but they soon disappeared. About 50 to 40 years ago the real settlements began. There were more people there then than there are now but the island has developed very much since then, as all the houses were shanties and there were hardly any trees and no roads. They do not have running water or electric light systems as a community but some families have private plants and running water, although a very few. There is a local telephone system and indirect telegraph service. A ferry boat makes four trips a day

in winter and three in summer. Mail and freight are brought over daily except Sunday on a steamboat which goes to three other nearby islands also.

Farming and fishing are the two chief industries. Fishing has been and still is quite prosperous. Farming was the biggest and most profitable industry until the depression. Tomatoes and peppers along with eggplant and squash are the chief winter crops. The tomatoes they raise are among the best in the country. Watermelons, cowpeas, okra, and pumpkins are chief summer crops. Almost three-fourths of the island was under cultivation until the Depression came but now only an acre or two is farmed by one man. There are a few other industries that come and go such as in the last two years people have been selling shells to Miami dealers to make trinkets out of.

There are some groves on the island which year before last raised the best fruit in Florida but the next year it was very poor. They have one large general store where you can get almost anything you want. In the winter time lots of tourists come to this island. There are three hotels, all of which have electricity. One has private bathrooms and the other two have a general bathroom.

The managers of these hotels are very genial and will do almost anything for your pleasure. The hotels are all on the water where you can go in swimming anytime you want to. If you want to go fishing you may go to any of the docks to fish or you can hire a guide to take you out in a boat for half a day or all day or at night if you choose. If you are a collector of shells you can go shelling, for Sanibel has the third best shelling beach in the world. It also has a very large variety of marine life which many scientists from all over America come to study. Every Saturday night in the winter and on special occasions, too, they have a dance which is usually by a Victrola but sometimes by an orchestra. In the summer time it is cooler here than any place else but the mosquitoes and sandflies are so bad that tourists could not have a good time. Most of the people that come down there in the winter have enough money to go anywhere they want to, so it is the charming people, the excellent climate and surroundings that bring them.

An island road in simpler times

Sanibel since the Depression hit it has not been quite as active or as pretty as before but still it is beautiful. The main road of the island is lined on both sides by tall Australian pines with small cocoanut trees set in between.

Occasionally you find hibiscus bushes along it, too. About six years ago there was kept a solid bed of periwinkles along this road and you can still see in many places large beds of them. The Spanish bayonet or yucca plant when it blooms is a marvelous sight to behold with its white spiral bunch of blossoms high up in the air.

All the growth on Sanibel is extremely pretty. One of the reasons for this is that it is situated near the tropics but still has enough temperate climate to make a climate well suited to wild growth. It also is a bird sanctuary. If you will go to the fields and hide yourself, in a few hours will be see around a hundred species of birds most of which are quite tame. The flocks of wild ducks that come there every winter are tame to a certain extent and will let you come very near them before flying up. The stately pelican when flying in the evening to the rookeries is a grand spectacle. Sanibel is noted for its exquisite sunsets of which no two resemble each other at all as do most sunsets.

Sanibel is an island of beauty and charm. If you want to have a good time next winter come down to Sanibel and you will remember those days the rest of your life.

Sanibel – all of Lee County – was a real frontier when my parents came here, in the sense that it was just being settled. People carried guns and occasionally would have a friendly argument where they split each other's heads open. It was a rough cowboy county. It wasn't as bad on Sanibel because there were a lot fewer people and a lot of them had church affiliations. There was law, but it was more like out in the west.

I know: I was raised here from the first days of life and have been here ever since except for time in school, the Army during World War II, and a couple of brief and failed attempts to find a career. Sanibel is my home, and this is where I have stayed.

CHAPTER 1
BEFORE MY TIME

THE BEGINNING

I can't think of anything more fitting than beginning with when I was born. The thing about farmers is the first born is usually born at home and the later children are born at hospitals. It was exactly the opposite in my family.

Lee Memorial Hospital on Victoria Street

My brother Sam always claimed my brother John and I were not true island natives because we were born in Fort Myers in Lee Memorial Hospital when it was an old wooden hospital on Victoria Street. I'm the oldest, born April 25, 1921; John was born October 9, 1922; and Sam was born January 29, 1924.

But the story goes back before I was born, as everyone's story does .

It started when our family first came to Sanibel. Daddy came in the summer of 1894 when he was 21 years old; Mother's family came in the summer of 1895. One of the first things that comes to mind when I think about what it was like for them is how they wore those stiff collars and heavy coats! Women looked like they were clothed for the North Pole even when they went swimming. Men would go fishing with stiff collars and heavy wool coats. Most clothing was just sponged off in those days because it was wool. When I was a kid, bathing suits were made of scratchy heavy wool with straps and took forever to dry out. But you became acclimated to the heat. Nature gradually gets cooler and gradually gets hotter, giving your body and mind time to adjust.

My father, Frank Bailey

My mother, Annie Mead Matthews, prior to her marriage to my father

Why come to Sanibel? Well, why did anyone go out west? To start a new lease on life. My father's older brother had run down the family tobacco business, and Daddy's father died when Daddy was 12 years old. There was no railroad so you came to the Caloosahatchee and couldn't cross it. A Rev. George Barnes had a church here and that had a lot to do with why they chose Sanibel. Uncle Ernest came down first, the summer before they moved, to see what it was like.

My family's move to Sanibel is really no different from the gold miners who picked up and headed off to the unknown to make their living. In fact, Daddy's father was in the gold rush in California. How he went out there I'm not sure, but when he came back, the story goes that he crossed the Isthmus of Panama on the back of a mule. There was no canal in those days of course. And he went around Cape Horn in South America. He didn't make a killing in the gold mining business, to say the least. He used what gold he did find to make a ring which my daughter Jane has now. That's quite a family heirloom to have and we're so happy to pass these things along to our children. He also came back with two or three seashells too; I don't know how he picked them up. You could tell they weren't Sanibel shells but most likely from a South American beach, or perhaps a California beach. I believe those pictures are lost now, as are too many of those old pictures. It's a shame.

Uncle Ernest

I think on both sides of the family, ol' John Barleycorn had a little to do with coming to Sanibel – to get away from drinking. Drinking was pretty acceptable in those days, even more than it is now – not for women, but it was for men. Uncle Ernest was not too addicted to staying close to work, though. He was the adventurous type. He went to Cuba in 1898 to 1901, approximately, and farmed there for a year or two to see whether he could do a good job there. He couldn't get in World War I as a soldier so he got in the YMCA and ended up on the battlefields of France. On Mother's side of the family, her father liked to tipple a little bit. But when you come right down to it, I'm not entirely sure of all the reasons that caused them to come to Sanibel. We can't find any connection to other Baileys beyond my father's daddy in Virginia. I think a lot of records were burned when the Yankees came through.

Another thing that may have had some impact on bringing Daddy down to Sanibel was my Aunt Alice – Daddy's sister and one of two girls in Daddy's family. She married a man from Cincinnati named Garvey. The Garvey Brothers had all kinds of groves in Florida when Aunt Alice moved here. Her husband was alive in 1919 when Daddy got

The label for one of my grandfather's chewing tobacco brands

married; I know because he's in the pictures I've seen, but I don't know how long he lived after that. During my lifetime, though, Aunt Alice was a widow and she lived in a house on the west side of Whiskey Creek – all orange groves and bamboo, it was. They owned groves in Alva too.

Daddy was born in Richmond, Virginia, in 1873 and was the youngest of nine children, seven of whom lived. His father was in the tobacco business, manufacturing chewing tobacco and snuff. Two of the brands were called Bailey's Comfort and another called Pride of the West. Family lore claims Samuel C. Bailey, Daddy's older brother, mismanaged and lost the tobacco company. I think there was a little too much John Barleycorn there, too.

My grandfather moved to Covington, Kentucky, across the river from Cincinnati, in 1879 when Daddy was six years old. He went into business there until he died in 1885. He had a brokerage tobacco business with a warehouse. Daddy never handled the tobacco in the field – it was the leaf tobacco after it came to market and already cured by the time he got it.

Daddy, although he was most definitely a Floridian, began his life in Virginia where he lived until age six when he moved with his family to Covington, Kentucky. His father died when he was 12; he was the youngest of nine children, seven of whom lived, and there was a span of 15 years between the eldest and the youngest. There were about three years between Uncle Ernest and Daddy. He finished his schooling in Kentucky and worked for a time as a clerk in a rolling mill. Daddy moved to Florida when he was 21. He just felt like his roots were in Virginia, and his father and mother were buried there, as well as a Confederate soldier who died in their home. I don't

Bailey's Comfort was the other brand of tobacco my family manufactured

know that whole story; there's a name on the stone but it's so deteriorated you can't read it. That's one of the ways history gets lost and it's a shame. And of course, and perhaps most importantly, that's where my mother is buried.

It's hard to explain, impossible really, how someone else feels. Daddy moved away from Virginia as a very young boy but he had family history there. That was a very important thing to him, and it was more important back then than perhaps it is today. It wasn't disrespectful to Florida as far as he was concerned. In fact, at one time before Daddy got married, he and Uncle Ernest were thinking of going up to Virginia and buying a farm and moving back there. Something happened that they didn't go and instead decided to remain in Florida. It was just the two of them then and they could have done anything, and they stayed.

Daddy and his eight siblings had some distance in years between them. Peter, the second-oldest, worked for the State Department as a diplomat and died in Central America from

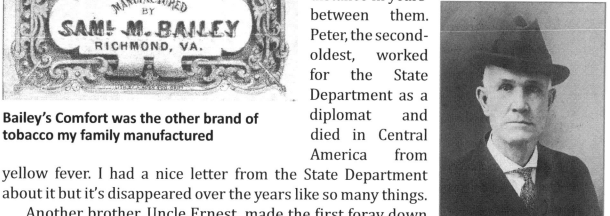

Uncle Harry

yellow fever. I had a nice letter from the State Department about it but it's disappeared over the years like so many things.

Another brother, Uncle Ernest, made the first foray down to Sanibel to see what was going on. The family was connected with the Episcopal Church and seemed to know a lot of

The Barnes family

bishops. Rev. George Barnes, who founded Casa Ybel, was from that neck of the woods and he apparently indirectly played a role in bringing Uncle Ernest and Daddy down here. Daddy had been working as a shipping clerk of some sort in a rolling mill – that's a steel mill that actually rolls out the steel – after the demise of the tobacco business, but I don't know what Uncle Ernest was doing.

As I said, I don't really know exactly why they decided to come down here; these have to be assumptions on my part. You take things for granted sometimes about your family's beginnings. That's one reason I wanted to write this book.

Nevertheless they decided they wanted to come to Sanibel and so they picked up lock, stock and barrel, and they came. I don't know if they went back and forth at first between Kentucky and Sanibel, but they settled in pretty quickly on the island into a house near where the Bait Box is today on Periwinkle Way. It was a two-story red house and it was still there when I was a kid. Daddy used to tell a funny story about that house. People were a lot more modest in those days – and there was a rainstorm, and there was Daddy standing under the eaves of his house in his birthday suit with a cake of soap taking a shower. There was a woman standing on her porch and he got out of there quick. In those days, more than 100 years ago, that was quite something different. He probably hadn't had any water in two weeks and maybe hadn't had a bath in a month, maybe two, and he couldn't stand it anymore.

DADDY AND HIS BROTHERS GET SETTLED

The Bailey Homestead in its original state

What is known today as the Bailey Homestead on Periwinkle Way was built in 1896 by R.H. Parks, who came to the island In 1880. A Rev. Andrew Wiren, who owned the land, had 150 acres and is buried near She Sells Sea Shells, also on Periwinkle Way. Daddy and Uncle Ernest each owned half of the homestead and there was never any mortgage on the house. That was one thing Daddy didn't believe in, mortgaging his home. Everything was that way, split equally between Daddy and Uncle Ernest. In fact, Daddy and Uncle Harry both got married in 1919. When Uncle Harry got married to a school teacher, he got part of the land that is Roadside City Park today and built a house on it. It's located where Three Crafty Ladies used to be, on the westernmost corner of land owned by the Sanibel-Captiva Conservation Foundation. Before my memories begin, Uncle Harry sold the house to the county (and it has been in government hands ever since, now the city of Sanibel) and moved to Fort Myers. He and his wife never had any children.. But I don't see Uncle Harry's name anywhere on any documents. In my memory, he was living in Fort Myers. I don't remember him being on the island at all.

When Daddy died and Uncle Ernest was still alive, my two brothers and I inherited Daddy's half of the house, and Uncle Ernest owned the other half. He always referred to the house as the "Smudge Pot" because of the mosquito repellant pots that were used back then. He had all kinds of crazy sayings and things like that.

But Uncle Ernest was half-owner of everything along with my father. The homestead land may have been deeded to my grandmother, Mary White Beers Bailey. My grandfather, Samuel

Mary White Beers Bailey, my grandmother

Major Bailey, was born in 1825 and died in 1886; he moved from Kentucky to Virginia in 1879. He had been an ambulance driver in the Confederate Army. After my grandfather's death, my father took devoted care of his mother. He also faithfully wrote his sister, Sarah Robertson (her husband was Victor Robinson, who published a commercial newspaper) in Berkeley, California once a week throughout the 1940s. He was very dedicated to them.

Daddy was very old-fashioned about taking care of his mother. His father died in 1879 when he was six years old, and his mother died in 1913. Sam said that Daddy's mother asked him to promise to take care of Uncle Ernest. Along about the same time, Daddy's elder brother, Samuel Major Bailey Jr., up in Covington, Kentucky died. When Daddy went up to bury him one of Daddy's nephews came around looking for his inheritance. He'd never been around to help his father or see him when he was sick. Daddy just handed him the doctor bills as if to say, "Here's the inheritance." Of course, Daddy had already paid those bills, but he never saw that relative again. I understand that arm of the family is in Cincinnati but we never again heard from that branch of the family tree.

My uncles Harry and Ernest were both talented in many ways, even though some claimed Ernest was allergic to work. Uncle Harry, who was six years older than Uncle Ernest, was a stenographer and took shorthand. Sam said all the women liked Uncle Ernest, although he never went out on a date in all the time I knew him.

Uncle Ernest worked at the store but would take off traveling from time to time. Daddy could see that I got interested in the store, fixing it up and working hard. We wanted the business to continue. About all Uncle Ernest did by this time was get in the way. We spent

Uncle Ernest in his older years

a lot of time laughing about his exploits. I think I got paid $100 a month but I had room and board at Daddy's. There was no money there but he had a lot of land. Uncle Ernest got some land Daddy owned to buy his share of the store. In those days we would have described the land "west of the subdivision." We know it today as Sanibel Shores, located along the Sanibel River on Donax Street and Junonia Street. All he didn't own was where the Holiday Inn is now located on Middle Gulf Drive, which I think is where my mother stayed when she first came here – just a piece of land with a home on it, or you might call it a structure: four rooms, windows everywhere, and most with a porch.

We kids were kind of boisterous with Uncle Ernest and he got shoved around, so to speak, although never physically. We would make noise when he was trying to read. In the summer Sam and I used to play ping pong on the dining room table while Uncle Ernest was in the next room trying to read. We knew we were disturbing him. John in particular gave Uncle Ernest a hard time. You look back and know you didn't realize what you were doing. For some reason, John had no use for Uncle Ernest and he was very obvious about it, was very non-communicative. But Uncle Ernest never yelled at us for our behavior.

Uncle Ernest had a lot of quirks and left us with a lot of good stories and memories. For example, he knew a smattering of French. Apparently they had a maid one time named Jenny Roan. Instead of eating her food she would put it aside to save. Uncle Ernest used to say, "I'm going to Jenny Roan it," meaning he was setting aside food. I was in my 20s before I realized that wasn't French for "putting it aside." But words were important to our parents, and we had to be respectful at all times. When I was growing up, Daddy told me you don't use the word "belly" – that while it's a perfectly good Anglo-Saxon word, you just don't use it in polite society; it was slang. We weren't allowed to use words like "guy" or "yeah."

I remember people asking Daddy, "What's Ernest doing these days?" and Daddy would answer, " He's not doing anything, he's writing. Want to know what he's writing? He's writing me a letter asking for money." But Uncle Ernest loved opera and read the encyclopedia like you would read a novel. And after his attempt at farming in Cuba, he's the one who decided there were no prospects there.

None of the Baileys of my father's generation went to college. They all graduated from high school and they all knew more from their high school educations than the average college graduate knows today. Uncle Ernest claimed he never read the funny papers, but we kids would start discussing something about Dick Tracy and make a mistake, and he'd correct us. Daddy would say things in Latin, although he didn't study as much as Uncle Ernest. I never heard Daddy make a mistake in his English, and he retained everything he read. People often came up to me and said, "Oh, your father was a professor at Princeton," or "I remember your Uncle Ernest, he was a professor somewhere." I'd say, "No, they probably could have done it, but they didn't."

Uncle Ernest was rather odd to say the least and led a quite different life from other people. He spoke with a southern Virginia accent. He didn't have a regular job and traveled to New York and acted in Hollywood. He was out at the Pasadena Playhouse several times acting before 1935. A lot of people know Uncle Ernest sunbathed in the nude, and in a very strange position: on his stomach with his rear end up in the air. He would surround himself with cardboard boxes for privacy but if they blew down, he didn't care. He thought sunbathing in this position prevented colon cancer. When we were kids, Frank Stegmen and Ben Fister of the Island Inn would throw cold water on Uncle Ernest while he was sunbathing, and somehow we Bailey boys would get blamed for it.

People had it rough on Sanibel during The Depression

I remember when Uncle Ernest came back in December 1934, the next night was the first time I had ever seen icicles. My mother used to tell me about living in Duluth, Minnesota, where they had double panes in the windows and they would draw in the ice on the windows. I didn't believe any of it. But there were icicles three feet long hanging off the water tank in our backyard, which was overflowing. Ice had formed on the grass in a patch as big as a conference table. That was quite a blow to the island; it was a terrible freeze. People were having a hard enough time during the Depression.

Daddy told me he had actually seen a few flakes of snow on Sanibel after the freeze of 1895 – a terrible freeze with ice and snow, and the citrus industry took a horrible beating. Near the coast we were better off than inland Florida. I've seen it snow flurry here since then. It must have been 1958 when we had such a terribly cold winter. Morning after morning I'd get up and the entire field outside would be just hoary white with frost. I remember Johnny Wakefield was living on Captiva but was originally from Worcester, Massachusetts, one of those winters and saw some snow on the street in Fort Myers. Now, Johnny liked to drink so he decided not to say anything to anybody because they would just say he'd been drunk. So he went into a place to eat and he was sitting there and some other guy got up enough nerve to mention the snow and Johnny said, "Boy, I'm sure glad to hear that."

Daddy's first job was hauling watermelons for one of the farmers who was already established here for two cents each, and he made more money than the rest of the haulers. It's become a bit of a famous story around the island how the other haulers couldn't figure out how Daddy was making more money; after all, you could only haul so many watermelons in a day. Well, they used wagons that had seats in them, and Daddy removed the seats and walked beside the wagon. This allowed him to fit more watermelons in the place where the seats had been removed. Watermelons were hauled to the wharf to be shipped. Things were different in my time: watermelons were just raised locally and we didn't ship them anymore.

That's the kind of person Daddy was all his life. He'd think of things like that. Any time he saw an opportunity to do something in a better way, he took advantage of it.

This is the way they started out, these island pioneers – with absolutely nothing. They almost didn't have enough to eat, yet they managed eventually to do very well.

DADDY ACQUIRES THE STORE, FARMS THE LAND

Some time after that, Daddy must have worked for a man named John Geraty who had some kind of a store down on Jane Matthews' wharf (she was no relation to the Matthews family that became part of the Bailey family). Daddy acquired that store in 1899; it's unclear exactly how. He knew that the island needed somebody to order things for people. Boats

Daddy bought the store at the end of Matthews' wharf before 1899

ran down from Punta Gorda – people were still getting supplies out of Punta Gorda then; there was no railroad in Fort Myers. In fact, there was nothing in Fort Myers at that time. I don't know how often the boats came down. There was a run boat – that's what the fishermen called it, but it was an ice boat and a fish boat. Its primary purpose was to supply all these fish houses isolated out in the water with no connection at all to the land.

Cuban smacks – small fishing vessels – would come to these waters, but the Cubans didn't really interact with islanders. For the most part, they anchored and never docked. There used

Cuban fisherman often came to our local waters.

to be six or eight of them in the harbor for shelter sometimes even when there weren't any storm warnings. They wouldn't stay there because they had to go where the fish were. It was different when a storm was coming, though. The barometer is what everybody went by. As soon as it started to drop – if it reached 27 that was bad news – the Cubans headed for the nearest shelter. Many of them couldn't swim, so they came ashore and stayed. In the late '20s, seven or eight of them stayed at our house. They helped Mother mop up the water all night. Most of them were good people. Later, after Daddy died, I would have them in the packing house. They never stole a thing even though there were plenty of loose items in there. Whoever was in charge had me check things over before they left. They stayed at the lighthouse, too, and probably other people's houses.

Daddy used to claim that the cook was really in charge of those Cuban smacks. Sam and John got on those smacks but I never did. The bait wells had big holes that allowed water to come up to the same level inside the boat as outside the boat. And they had no refrigeration. They used that water to keep the fish alive.

The fish houses were bigger than the office I use today and would use fifteen or twenty 300-pound blocks of ice each week (of course, they weren't 300 pounds by the time they got here due to melting). The boat would pick up fish and replenish the ice and bring supplies. There were fish houses all through the harbor with big walk-in ice boxes. Local fishermen would bring in their catches, which would be shipped north. The author Randy Wayne White was a fishing guide here and he used to sell his catch to a restaurant on Rabbit Road where Doc Ford's is now.

There were two kinds of ice — one not very sanitary that was made from dirty water and was used for the fish houses — and clear ice. Even back in the 1940s and '50s people still had ice boxes. I used to haul ice for some of them. In a home there would be an ice box that included another, separate compartment in which you put your food.

The other water was probably sulfur water. It was dirty looking but for the purpose it was used in the fish houses – to cool the ice boxes – what's the difference? Of course there was no refrigeration in the flat cars used to ship citrus nor in the cars for fish, so they would put these 300-pound blocks of ice, not one block but many, on both ends of the cars. I remember seeing them load the huge blocks from the ice plant in Fort Myers. On the Punta Gorda boat, ice came from the plant there. By the time I came along, the ice came from a plant in Fort Myers.

The mail came in from Fort Myers and was handled by two different paid people. When the mailbag got to the dock, the bags were locked and went to the Post Office for the postmaster to open. By that time we had all kinds of people delivering mail, including Webster "Webb" Shanahan. When you carry a locked mail bag, I think you call those "star routes." Once off the mail boat they'd take those star routes to the post office. We had a dozen mail carriers to carry the open mail bags and the rest of the mail was locked up. It must've been a universal lock. It wasn't his job, but Pat Murphy helped sort the mail. That's what people did in those days, pitched in and helped each other, and Pat could only work 10 a.m. to 2 p.m. because of the boat's schedule. He was originally the mail carrier then later carried the locked mailbags from the boat to the Post Office.

Webb Shanahan

Will Reed was the postmaster and he died while I was away. There weren't that many people here to go to the Post Office. We had a rural mail delivery. Sometimes you would just leave a letter without postage on it and the rural carrier would take care of it. You could put two cents on and he would mail it, or put five cents on and he would bring you back three cents.

Will Reed

I remember one rumor. The mail boat captain, Palmer Ladd, came back from Captiva and said he heard I was moving off the island. I said, "I'm not even going on vacation!" He got mad at me because he didn't believe me. If you keep your ears open and your mouth shut, you can hear almost anything on Sanibel and Captiva.

There was another post office on the island at Wulfert, where there was also a little store. The people who lived there used to come down to our store periodically in an old Model A sedan and buy gas. You didn't need much gas then – there weren't many places to drive. Where were you going to go?

Meanwhile, the store evolved. You know that song *Sixteen Tons* about how a coal miner ends up owing his soul to the company store? It wasn't severe like that, not at all, but Daddy did have charge accounts. Going through those accounts now, I'm amazed at some of the ledgers that

The store after the 1926 move

say, "I can't pay, here's $5." When I first came to work for Daddy, people owed all kinds of money and that was tough for Daddy, but it made the community better and helped it grow.

Daddy's desk was never neat — neither is mine! But we get the work done.

Daddy was serving people and meeting a real need for island folks. But even in a huge community, which Sanibel decidedly was not, when a business goes out of business, everybody feels it. And selling on credit was bad, because Daddy had mouths to feed and a business to keep afloat.

Daddy took advantage of any opportunity and though he never said it, I could observe that he was involved in sharecropping, which was a big deal throughout the south.

Basically it's a system under which a non-farmer furnishes all the necessities to farm the land — mule, plow, seed, and fertilizer— and then the sharecropper furnishes all the labor. The sharecropper is really a tenant farmer on the owner's land who gives a share of the crops raised to the landowner in lieu of rent. Sharecroppers were both white and black men.

Daddy farmed until well into the 1940s with no mechanized equipment

Farmers can raise more crops than they can harvest. We used to have to get people in from the outside to pick the crops. Then when all was said and done, I don't know how they split up the harvest, by what percentages. If a farmer had absolutely nothing but his hands – that is, his labor -- to offer, it would be a little different from somebody who had something but just needed some help. The white and black sharecroppers were not treated differently financially as far as I know. Mother tried to talk Daddy out of sharecropping and he said later he should have listened to her because he lost money, because people left the island.

There was risk involved. At the end of the season, if it was a bad crop or the market dropped or the farmer didn't have much and the person who put up the money had a lot of debt, the system didn't work. Sometimes when you had two crops in one year, you might make a bunch of money on the first one and lose it all on the next one.

Daddy had a worker named Ed Sherman – originally he did anything, any job that was required. Like most people on Sanibel, his primary job was farming. He worked for Daddy at the turn of the century, then went to New Mexico for 10 years or so, then came back. By the time my brothers and I came along, he lived across the street and took care of our mules and chickens and the grove. He was a farmer type, a farm hand. A couple of times he quit and went to sharecropping, but he would always come back to work for Daddy. But he'd never say he was back – he would just show up and go to work. Finally Daddy said, "If you leave again, you cannot come back, do you understand that?" "Yes, sir," Ed answered. Then Daddy found him putting a piling down on some property on a dock that Daddy owned. Daddy asked Ed, "Who are you working for?" As matter-of-fact as can be, Ed answered Daddy, "You."

Farming is a hard business, but Daddy was quite successful at that time and he made money.

MY PARENTS' COURTSHIP AND MARRIAGE

Meanwhile, Daddy had been courting Annie Mead Matthews for some time but they didn't get married until 1919 when Daddy was 46 years old, four years after Grandmother Bailey died. At this time, Daddy was very well off (a few years after that, he was anything but). I don't know how Uncle Ernest reacted to Daddy's marriage. He seemed to have every respect for Mother. Daddy asked her if she would like another house someplace for them and let Uncle Ernest continue to live at the homestead. As I said, Uncle Ernest and my father owned everything together. If his name wasn't on something, it didn't make any difference as far as they were concerned. Sam and I did a little of that, too. At that stage Daddy could have built another house, but Mother said no. She knew how much Daddy wanted to stay at the homestead.

I'm not sure why it took my father so long to get married, except that he was caring for his mother and then settling her estate. The traditions of the time said you didn't marry quickly, I suppose. Daddy was 12 years older than Mother. In fact, his mother-in-law was closer to his age than his wife. Mother was only a little girl of nine when her family came to Sanibel.

Mother and Daddy's courtship was filled with dancing. Daddy had the big two-story packing house (which would blow down in 1935). The upper story was living quarters, and the lower story was the packing house. I don't remember much about it except playing up there a few times. During my lifetime it was more of a junk collection than a packing house. But it did have a wooden floor.

I've been told they didn't have to

Mother and Father on their wedding day, 1919

announce they were having a dance – they just started cleaning the place in preparation and when people saw the dust flying out, everyone knew there was going to be a dance that night. They must have had dances elsewhere, too. People on the island were very

21

social in those days. There was no radio, no TV — thank God — and no telephones.

In those days they used dance cards – you had to ask a lady to dance and get on her dance card if she had an opening. I never filled out a dance card, but I've seen some of them. I seem to remember dance cards might even have been filled out ahead of time, before the dance. Apparently some people kept them for some reason. And it was always "Miss," never first names; we were very formal. People weren't as free and easy with the first names. With elders, if it wasn't Mr. or Mrs., it might be Aunt or Uncle. Today, you know, you meet someone and you call them Mary or Jack. In those days, people could know each other for 30 years and still call them Mrs. Bailey and Mrs. Matthews.

Early picture of The Matthews

Back to Sanibel in Daddy's time, a lot of Daddy and Mother's courtship was dancing at the Matthews Hotel, where a lot of the island socializing took place. Among those were people with very diverse backgrounds and fields of work, plus there were the winter visitors, some of whom were quite well off.

For example, a lot of people down here were Georgia people. Grandmother Matthews would invite them to come up to The Matthews in the "evening" to play cards. But her idea of "evening" was not the same as theirs. They would show up at two o'clock in the afternoon! Well if a man worked on a farm, 2 p.m. was evening since he started work so early in the morning. It made for an embarrassing situation because people at The Matthews weren't prepared for guests at two o'clock and were dressed casually. That mattered a lot in those days. It would feel humiliating to a hostess if people might see her in her casual clothes, perhaps with a hole that hadn't been mended. That might be hard to imagine today, when young people put holes in their clothes on purpose. Back then, it didn't make any difference how faded your clothes were as long as they were clean with no holes. Those were the days when people even darned socks.

THE MATTHEWS FAMILY

My mother's family came to Sanibel in 1895. I think they came in sailboats from Punta Gorda but maybe they were steamboats. They landed at Reeds Landing; that's where the Post Office was at the time. Today it would be a few hundred yards west of where Dixie Beach Boulevard meets the bay. People drove everywhere with a horse and wagon, and the fiddler crabs would be so thick on the island, it looked like the road was moving. My mother thought they were spiders and she was not impressed. What's more, Mother had never seen a palm tree and expected a tiger to jump out from behind one any minute, and that was because of a children's story from 1899, The Story of Little Black Sambo. In it, tigers chase each other around a tree until they are turned into butter. It became somewhat controversial for obvious reasons, but it was very popular at the time and we all knew it. This is the story:

> **The Story of Little Black Sambo** is a children's book by Helen Bannerman first published in 1899. Sambo is a South Indian boy who encounters four hungry tigers and surrenders his colorful new clothes, shoes, and umbrella so they will not eat him. The tigers chase each other around a tree until they are reduced to a pool of melted butter; Sambo then recovers his clothes and his mother makes pancakes of the butter. The story was a children's favorite for half a century until the word Sambo came to be considered a racial slur.
>
> *(Source: Wikipedia)*

Much later, my wife June, who's from Winnipeg, Canada, thought it was comical to see a cow under a palm tree, but that was a common occurrence for us.

The Nutt family at The Gables

Now "Gray Gables" as it is today

There were boarding houses and places to stay available on Sanibel even in those early days. A family named Nutt owned The Gables, which was later re-named Gray Gables. Laetitia Ashmore Nutt, the mother, ran a small boarding house there and had three daughters. If you stayed six nights and paid every night, the seventh night was free. But you couldn't wait to the end to pay; you had to pay every night. The story was that she was "tight," but I never knew that for a fact.

Laetitia Nutt in her older years

I heard but was never sure that Mrs. Nutt's husband came from Mississippi and died in the War Between the States. At any rate, all I knew was that Mr. Nutt was gone. She may have been a widow when she moved here.

Her children all became school teachers. Cordie Nutt taught Sunday School to younger children; Nannie Nutt married a man and moved with him to California but returned to Sanibel many years later; and Lettie Nutt also taught school (Lettie was the one to give us the Shakespeare volumes). Cordie could tell some marvelous stories. As a boy, she looked to me like she was 200 years old, the way older people do to young children.

In those days it seemed to me there was more travel than there is today but of a different type: people stayed longer and brought all their clothes in big trunks. This definitely called for boarding houses and hotels to spring up.

Apparently the way Granny Matthews got into the boarding house business was that some of the relatives would come to visit. Before long, friends of friends came and it evolved from there. I have to assume some couldn't pay for it and had to make some special arrangement to pay with money or in kind. Granny's business evolved into the hotel The Matthews, and in 1936 became the Island Inn which it remains today.

The Barracks at The Matthews

Granny Matthews' family at that time consisted of her husband, Will; my mother, Annie Mead; Aunt Douglas; Aunt Charlotta, also known affectionately by the nickname Chebum; Uncle Clark (during my lifetime, he never lived there at all; he was a balloonist in WWI). Grandpa Matthews I remember slightly but I really didn't know him. He had cancer.

Granny Matthews on her beautiful gulf-front property

Interior views of The Matthews

Chebum with a neighbor

Here's where the nickname "Chebum" came from, although it doesn't seem to make much sense. She was trying to learn to drive a Model T and when something was difficult she would stick her chin out with her lower teeth kind of protruding. I'm not sure what that had to do with "Chebum," but that's what we called her then and it caught on. Maybe because she also did not like to be called "Aunt" — anything but "Aunt"! In those days she was very self-conscious about her age. Since we did not use first names in our family that might have been one reason to find her a nickname.

Sometime after The Matthews was established, Granny and some of her daughters went summers to work at the Glenburnie Inn resort in Lake George in New York's Adirondack Mountains, a town with many resorts. They ran the summer resort's dining room for quite a number of summers. The resort later burned down. Aunt Douglas got married then and moved away; her husband was a professor at Temple University in Pennsylvania.

Aunt Janie Matthews, who was no relation to the Bailey-Matthews family, owned the dock on which Daddy's original

Granny Matthews with her daughter - my mother - Annie Mead Matthews

25

store sat. I have no idea how Granny paid Aunt Janie for the property on which The Matthews was located; it could be she left the property to Aunt Janie in her will. That transaction took place around the turn of the century. The big three-story building known as The Barracks wasn't built until 1913-1918. A fire eventually burned the house down. This means the Island Inn was founded somewhere around 1915 as The Matthews, quite a while after 1895 as the Island Inn claims today.

The Matthews offered simple living on a pristine, quiet beach

The Matthews was absolutely beautiful, and in an ideal location on a pristine, quiet beach. But it was still simple living, especially by the standards of some of the wealthier guests who came to stay. The rooms were just square rooms. The bathroom facilities, rugged by today's standards to say the least, were in the corner of the room with just a board across with a wash bowl, a pitcher and a soap dish. On the floor underneath were two thunder jugs, or chamber pots – a small one and a bigger one. The plumbing was orchard-style, which is to say, outhouses. The term "orchard plumbing" refers to outhouse toilets, with a couple of stalls in each one. These were located quite a distance from the house, for obvious reasons. The clothes closets were like bookcases without shelves but instead with a bar across the top and a curtain across it.

That was the way things were built in those days. It was probably quite elaborate for the time for an isolated barrier island like Sanibel. Yet people who had money would come down here and use these facilities, which were primitive by the standards of their wealthy lifestyles, simply because they loved the island. I'm sure they were used to much more luxury. It's amazing, really, and speaks to the immense appeal of Sanibel.

The beach in front of The Matthews

In 1913, Granny started building The Barracks and it

was completed in 1914. Any kind of indoor plumbing was still 25 years away. I can't say these are firm dates, but it's in the right range.

There was a fire in The Matthews in the building where Mother was sleeping. She escaped at night with just her nightgown on, so after that, night after night my mother would make my father get out of bed because she thought she smelled smoke. He'd say, "Honey, there's no fire but I'll go." Other than that, I never heard a whole lot about the fire there.

Granny Matthews stands with the Island Inn station wagon after she sold The Matthews

A man we called Pop Furneaux who was in his 80s insisted on living on the third floor but also insisted on having a rope in case there was a fire.

In the early 1930s, the inn would offer a fisherman's box lunch. Those guests would go out with fishing guides and could find a little beach on one of the islands and build a fire from driftwood, put lard in and fish, and there you were – paradise.

A lot of the homes that were there by the Island Inn are torn down now and have been replaced by condos. People would build homes adjacent to the inn and then eat their meals at the inn. Some of the houses that are still there today were built in my lifetime and had their own electricity, and in those days you could dig a shallow well or deep well and have fresh water. The water was hard as a rock, but it was fresh water. Later on they tried aerating it to get rid of the rotten egg smell; it helped a lot but it didn't get rid of all of the smell.

We had some people even in my time who were "snowbirds" as we call them today, but we never used that term. They were called "winter people." No self-respecting winter person would be caught dead on the island later than the first of April. They'd come around November first with their big steamer trunks and wardrobe trunks. There was a man named Curtis Perry who painted beautiful sunsets and always came down here for the winter. He stayed at the Island Inn in the same room every year and he was a financial contributor to the Community House along with the Woodrings, my family, and the Nutt sisters who donated the land.

THE ISLAND'S EARLY GROWTH

I never heard of anybody really suffering due to an emergency back before Sanibel was connected to the mainland. If you had an emergency, you telegraphed and the ferry would meet the ambulance, bring you over, and take you back. After Reeds Landing was destroyed in 1926, Kinzie Brothers took over the ferry and built a dock where our store was located. The only way you could get to the island was to swim or take a boat. People didn't come for weekends in those days – it would take a weekend just to get here!

Pauline examining our gulf-front property before we built our home

People did get medical help on the island, though. Louise Perry, who was no relation to Curtis the sunset painter, was a doctor, although everyone called her "Mrs." I believe she tried to breed junonias, and she did collect shells. She helped with all kinds of doctoring but we found out later she was an ophthalmologist. Still, she did fine; in fact, Lake Louise is named after her.

When I first got married, my wife Pauline and I were clearing a lot up on the beach to build our first house – that would be the cottage Sam called Honeymoon Cottage – and I accidentally hit her in the head with a grubbing hoe. I went to Esperanza Woodring and she took us in her boat to Punta Rassa where I borrowed a Jeep from a ferry employee, took Pauline into town, got her patched up, and brought her back. That was one way to go about getting medical care!

In the 1930s and '40s, there was a big Western Union office in Punta Rassa, and the little telegraph cable hut is still there. Two buildings were operators' homes. As a boy looking at it, it was fascinating to me. Later in the Army, I would go to radio school, strictly by coincidence. We used to build radios, big radios, there. The story goes that Sanibel was the first part of the continental U.S. to hear about the sinking of the *USS Maine* on February 15, 1898. Western Union and Daddy got together to use that cable to bring Western Union for Sanibel.

Daddy got the Western Union telegraph over here in approximately 1910. If you wanted to send a telegraph to Fort Myers, we had a wire phone and would read the telegraph over the phone, then they wired it to Tampa through the Punta Rassa hut that is still there today, and Tampa wired Fort Myers. Originally it was all done by voice in that way. Later we had a teletype machine.

There were two exceptions to our usual system: an emergency, say if somebody was sick; and the other was when you wanted to find out what the ball scores were. Maybe

Telegraph cable hut as it stands today in Punta Rassa

I'm "pulling a Sam here" – which is the term I use for exaggerating to make a good story because that's what Sam liked to do – but that's the way we always talked about it. I don't know how it worked. Sam enjoyed some of those things. He was a big baseball fan and would ask the girls he knew in the Fort Myers telegraph office to step outside and see if it was raining so he would know whether to go into town to play baseball that night, or just to get the baseball scores.

Western Union had a cable that went past Key West to Havana, but it went across Sanibel on its way to those places. Long before I was born they stopped using that cable and the newer cable went down the channel. This left the cable from Punta Rassa to Sanibel unused and inactive. This was before 1910.

During World War II the government spent money like crazy and put down another cable with a phone to the lighthouse. After the war, that single phone was moved up to the Casa Marina at the ferry landing (there's a home there now). People would line up to use that phone. Before that the only communication was Western Union or U.S. mail. This new telephone system operated just within the island. What we had was strictly a single line telephone. You'd crank a handle, which would cause a bell to ring on the other end. They had three to six dry cells and the chemistry in them gave you the voltage, not the size.

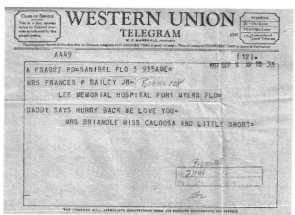
Telegram sent after the birth of Jane Bailey to Francis & Pauline

Daddy and J.N. Johnson (I'm sorry to say we called him Fatty) put in the telephone line — a relatively short pole and one metallic galvanized wire and insulator hooked up to the phones and grounded. When Lee County Electric Cooperative came over they also grounded their lines. As a result we got that A/C hum on the wire so we had to put up a second wire. We put a single phone on each end of the island and at first used that old Western Union cable for the on-island phone service only; you couldn't call from Sanibel to Fort Myers or anywhere else. It was strictly Sanibel-to-Sanibel telephone service. Telegraphs went straight to Tampa; today some of our mail still does that.

Then a man named Frank King came to me and said, "Let's start our own telephone system." I went to see my attorney (James Franklin, Jr., the son of the partner in today's Henderson Franklin firm), who didn't seem very receptive and I couldn't figure that out. The next day, the president, CEO, manager, and who knows who else from the telephone company (Inter County Telephone & Telegraph) were sitting in my office saying, "This could be our territory." They were afraid that if we got established they would have to buy us out to gain control of the Sanibel territory. I told him we wanted telephone service now, not next year. I didn't want to own or run a telephone company; I had enough problems. I just wanted to be able to use a telephone.

The result was that the island had three lines with six to eight people on each line, known as party lines. Some families, like the Ross Mayer family, had children who would leave the receiver off the hook. I'd yell into the phone, "Hang up the phone!" You couldn't use it; you were locked out. Eventually I'd be forced to drive down there and tell them to hang up the receiver. And some people of course would want to listen in.

They did away with the Western Union office at Punta Rassa and had a telephone line that ran from Punta Rassa to Fort Myers, so the telephone line on poles that ran from Fort Myers to Punta Rassa could then come across the cable to Sanibel. In those days it was the same communication but further away with one wire and a little more difficult.

Then we finally got the teletype machine but sometimes there were difficulties. I remember one Christmas Day when I was down at the store, there was a big fire at the Fort Myers ice plant. That plant was connected with the Florida Power & Light plant and their power

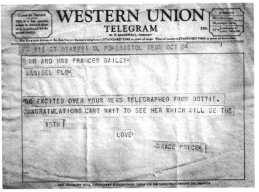

went out, so the teletype wouldn't work. So I sat there Christmas morning writing out telegrams until my fingers were numb.

The Rural Electrification Administration came to the island around 1940 (the electricity the homestead got in 1921 was direct current, 32 volts with a little generator to charge the batteries). When Lee County Electric Cooperative was doing its work, Uncle Ernest and Daddy were living and my brothers and I were in school. We wanted electricity on the island, of course, so we were trying to do everything we could to help LCEC. If crews were working late or something, they were always welcome to stay at our house. Uncle Ernest was also a trustee of LCEC.

LCEC's territory then included Captiva, Sanibel, Pine Island and North Fort Myers. It was called a cooperative in those days, just as it is today. There were two trustees from each of those four areas. Uncle Ernest represented Sanibel. When he died, I was appointed or elected, I forget which. Then LCEC started reducing the number of trustees; now there is one for both Sanibel and Captiva when we used to have two for each island. I served on there long enough, until they built the new building which is about their third.

Aerial view of Sanibel, 1940

HARD TIMES COME TO SANIBEL

Basically up until WWII Sanibel was a farming community. Stuff was shipped out of here to all parts of the U.S. mostly by boat, and the island was quite well known. The farmers sort of looked down their noses at people in the tourism business. Even the Matthews family looked at what became the Island Inn as a sideline. Granny just started it because it was a necessity, and she enjoyed it; she was the friendly, outgoing type. The island gradually grew into tourism. The rest was farming, but farming had deteriorated. There were

Farming on Sanibel ended.

some hotels, but they were insignificant compared to farming. Then the island evolved into a tourist resort.

Sanibel became a tourist resort and it remains so.

I can only think of one person on the island at that time who wasn't dependent on tourism, and that was Sammy Woodring, Ralph's half-brother. He was a commercial fisherman, although I guess even he was dependent on the tourists — but what he wanted from them was liquor. Sammy was a big bootlegger. Alcohol was forbidden in our house; my mother detested it. It was against the law so Daddy and Uncle Ernest didn't drink. Uncle Ernest used to talk about sherry all the time, saying things like, "This food would go good with sherry." Daddy was violently against drinking. Later, in the mid-1940s with restaurants springing up all over, there was a big controversy about having beer and about where it could be served. We didn't want it because it was close to our house. Some people just didn't want alcohol around.

Daddy was pretty successful up into the early 1920s. The first hurricane in 1921 — the year I was born, by the way — set farming back some; the one in 1926 even more. Florida experienced a boom-and-bust just like now: booming in the 1920s, then busted in the 1930s. You could go anywhere in Florida in those days and all you would see were fire hydrants and street signs because that's all that was left.

Uncle Harry standing in our lime grove

There had been farmers all over the place. Sanibel started booming soon after Daddy got here. In 1926 a lot of people left. When I was growing up there were abandoned houses all over the island. Some became occupied by colored folks and some by people from out west. Workers on the Hoover Dam would come here and sometimes they would stay two or three years; sometimes they had a whole bunch of kids, sometimes one or two in the school. I had a crush on one of the women in those families – her name was Margaret. These families never contributed a great deal to the lifestyle of the island but they were here and I remember them. Some of their houses burned down when we had grass fires. We used to have a lot of grass fires and our firefighting equipment was somewhat primitive.

Roughly in the mid-1920s my family spent three summers in North Carolina. The family would go for three or four months, and Daddy would come and go. Granny's husband died there in 1927. One year I remember distinctly Daddy was gone a month in July. That was the beginning of the planting season so he had to go back to Sanibel. But time doesn't mean a lot to a kid that age.

I have many memories of our times in North Carolina. The first house we stayed in had a porch swing on an open porch, and Mother used to make cottage cheese, with the cheese hanging up in a big ball. The second time we went we stayed in a house up on a hill. The garage was really just a roof with posts on the side and Sam got in the car, a big old Studebaker, and somehow the car was in neutral and the brake was off and it rolled down the hill in between the trees. It banged him up a bit. He was only 2½ years old!

The third North Carolina house was farther away. It had a run-down apple orchard with a stone wall around it. There was a hill behind it where we used to play. I remember there were red berries and I got them all over my hands and then – didn't I need to go to the bathroom! I ended up with itching you wouldn't believe. To this day, I get near any bush that looks like that bush, I'm gone! Poison ivy doesn't seem to bother me, but those red berries sure did.

There was a little town that had a railroad station that ran parallel to the shops. There was a gift shop, a grocery store, and a bunch of empty space. I went back when I was grown and they had made a playground and the gift shop was bolted up. I closed my eyes, though, and I could see 1926, 1927.

We had never had milk to drink up to that point. On Sanibel, we had powdered milk called KLIM ("milk" spelled backwards). The first time I had real milk, I had to run like heck to get to the edge of the porch and throw up. My body just wasn't used to it, I guess. Now there's so much done to milk these days, a calf wouldn't know what to do with it.

We would go to the railroad station and wave at the engineers. We loved doing that. Melrose Grade was a steep climb up to the station, and it took four engines, two in the front and two in the back, to pull the train up, that's how steep it was.

I don't remember being impressed by the different landscape as a boy. I remember being in bed and hearing the train whistle. To me it was just a wonderful sound off in the distance. There was a second whistle in my life at that time, though: Mother had a whistle, and when she blew it, you knew you'd better answer and tell her where you were, or else you'd better get home.

And then the Depression hit and there wasn't much going on in the way of traveling or anything, until sometime between 1932 and 1934. We decided to take a three-day trip throughout Florida, a mini-vacation. The only two things I distinctly remember are going to hotels and the guy at the desk would want $5 or so per person per night. Daddy would have a $5 bill and say, "Would you like this?" and nine out of 10 times, they accepted. And the other place I remember from that trip was Howey-in-the-Hills, a little town in the middle of the state. It started as a subdivision in the middle of the boom and of course flopped. There were two routes that were really just loose sand. I can't remember anything except the routes and apparently we got stuck. I don't know how we got out of there, I just remember being in there. It was quite a trauma.

On the shore of Little Lake Harris, about 37 miles from Orlando

At one time Daddy owned quite a lot of land. You don't like to say that because it makes people think you're rich. For the most part, the land was a drain to him rather than an asset because he was paying taxes on it.

The Baileys have been able at times to donate land for good purposes, and I would love to have been able to donate the homestead land but I couldn't do it – for the sake of my estate, my family and my eight children.

The Bailey-Matthews Shell Museum sits on eight acres my brothers and I donated.

My brothers and I contributed the land, eight acres, for the Bailey-Matthews Shell Museum on Sanibel-Captiva Road. There had been talk for years about building a shell museum – as far back as the 1940s. Many islanders had magnificent shell collections they wanted to donate. It just evolved; you have to start someplace. In early 1989, my two brothers and I deeded over the eight acres of land south of Sanibel-Captiva Road. We did it in honor of our parents. Our family has stayed involved, too, since donating the land. John's wife Sally was on the original board of directors. After Sally got off, I got on – twice, I think. Sam served on the board too. I think it's a good thing because for years shells and Sanibel were almost synonymous – they still are today. Shelling and fishing were what people came here for and, to a certain extent, the solitude.

The land for the Bailey Tract, part of Ding Darling, was 50 acres. Daddy did get some money for it – it was right in the middle of the Depression. I'm sure he would have liked to donate it but, simply put, couldn't afford to do it. Some other land on Beach Road was

The Bailey Tract in the "Ding" Darling Refuge

donated to the City of Sanibel for affordable housing (Community Housing & Resources). What we received in return for that donation was to have first choice, everything else being equal, for some of our employees to be able to live there. In other words, it gave our employees "points" that would move them higher on the waiting list for the Beach Road housing.

So land can make you money or lose you money. We donated when we were able, as I'm sure Daddy would have done. Back then, with the Depression plus the hurricanes, people left Sanibel in droves and a lot of people owed Daddy a lot of money. So some people would deed their land over instead of paying. Before 1921, Daddy and his brother were pretty successful. Uncle Ernest was in the habit of buying stuff, though, including land in New York. He would go off to Hollywood, California, for two to three months and even worked with Errol Flynn. He was supposed to be a half partner in the business but he wasn't participating.

Affordable housing came to Beach Road on land I was able to donate.

During that period, Daddy joined the Independent Grocers Alliance (IGA) and went to Biloxi, Mississippi, for a convention and I remember that's when I had my appendix out. In those days you didn't operate at the drop of a hat and Mother had to make a decision. Thank God she made it. I'd already had my tonsils out. Since these childhood surgeries, I've had so many operations I'm like a bionic man.

Daddy got more involved with the IGA, which doesn't really handle any merchandise per se. It is an advisory organization. But they have distributors. We had nothing to do with IGA from the mid-1930s to five years ago or so. Daddy couldn't afford to pay the fee. That's how tough things were in those days. Associated Grocers of Florida (AG) is a different organization. I've been on its board since 1972, and we've been buying groceries from them since 1962 or so. I'm still not the oldest in tenure on the board, there's one guy ahead of me, but I am the oldest in age. The other association is the National Grocers Association.

But here I go again, jumping around like a fly on a hot griddle. Back to my story.

So after the 1926 hurricane things were pretty slow. Things were pretty austere as far as taking vacations or even leaving the island. We used to go to the Island Inn and spend the summers up there. It was just five miles away but it was on the beach and it was Mother's home, and of course her sister and Granny were there.

There was still farming going on, and farmers were here trying to make a go of it, but compared to the past, it was just a drop in the bucket. The salt in the soil from the hurricane would eventually leach out of the soil with rain, but that takes time, and a lot of people couldn't afford the time.

KINZIE FERRY LANDING
1928-1939

The ferries were a big part of island life, of course, and kept operating no matter what else was happening on the island. Captain Leon used to let some of the children go up and steer *The Best*. You always overcorrected; you would turn around and look back at the wake. The wheelhouse was up a few steps, and there was a cabin in the back with U-shaped benches attached to the wall.

It was the *Gladys* we would ride most of the time, but also *The Dixie*. You could tell *The Dixie* because it had an eagle on top of the pilot house. It was white, and the front decks were where the freight was carried. The gang plank came into the dock for loading or else crews would just throw the freight on. Sometimes they brought mules across. The last time I saw that boat was 1935 or '36. It sank near the lighthouse.

We're on the *Gladys* in the picture of my brothers and me with Mother. In it, the three of us are pointing, but I don't know what we're pointing at. I suppose it's whatever our Aunt Kate told us to do. She was here on a visit and she was a very good photographer who became rather successful.

There was also the *Yankee Clipper* and *Rebel*, and sometimes the captain would let us ride with him. I rode the mail boat, too. Before the ferry boats, everything had to come on

steamships from Fort Myers. The steamships were still coming when I was a kid. In the very early part of the century, Kinzie Brothers got the mail contract and delivered the mail. They also had a side business harvesting oyster shells, which were used for all kinds of things.

The steamboats left Fort Myers, sometimes stopped in Punta Rassa, sometimes at Dixie Dock that Kinzie had near the lighthouse, then the Bailey Dock, then Reed's Landing where it unloaded the mail. Then it was on to St. James City, then Wulfert, and finally Captiva. Along the way, they unloaded passengers and freight. The main thrust of the trip, though, was the mail contract. On their way back, we loaded all our vegetables and other goods on the steamboats. Eventually Kinzie Brothers lost the mail contract to Singleton Brothers.

The ferry ran from Punta Rassa to Reed's Landing. The 1926 hurricane ruined everything, though. Kinzie built a dock at Bailey's and kept in there until 1936 or 1937 then moved it down further east to Ferry Road when the steamboat stopped running. They just had the ferry and the oyster shell business then.

Mother with Sam, me and John on the bow of the *Gladys*

CHAPTER 2
MY EARLY YEARS

LOSING MOTHER

In 1935 Mother died in June and in the fall I went away to school. Naturally those are things I remember very distinctly. Mother was wonderful. She was such a hard worker and really cared for us, not just in speech, but in the way she provided for us – always preparing proper meals, having us keep an early bed time and such. She really loved us and showed it in every way she possibly could. I was just 14 when she passed away. I remember her as an elegant, refined woman; my father worshiped her and would do anything for her.

We knew Mother wasn't well. She was always sickly in a way, with headaches, foot trouble, and other things, but she was not a complainer. Never. Mother didn't say much, and I wouldn't have known what cancer was anyway. People weren't as open then about medical things – and especially not with children. I found out when I was older that the surgeon had opened her up and sewed her right back up. She was just too riddled with cancer.

Every night when I saw a star in the sky, I would recite that child's chant that's supposed to be for happy things – "Star light, star bright ..." – but I would be wishing for Mother to get well, and I'd always make the same wish in my prayers at night.

Mother was in Fort Myers in the hospital and we boys were staying at the Island Inn. We knew that the last ferry left Punta Rassa at 4:30. I think it was in the middle of the day that Daddy showed up at the inn, but I know whenever it was, it was an unusual time for him to arrive because of the ferry schedule. He may have gotten someone to bring him over, a friend or a fisherman. But I was at the Island Inn in the old building. It had a door going out on the porch but also had two windows low to the ground, and I was standing at one of those windows. He came in and told us Mother had passed. We didn't expect it – everyone had told us she would be coming home. And I just cried and cried.

Mother with me, Sam and John

Daddy was not a very outwardly emotional person but I remember some very poignant instances after Mother's death.

For example, in spite of the fact he left Virginia when he was six years old, in many ways he never left emotionally. The only specific instruction he had in his will was he wanted to be buried in Hollywood Cemetery in Richmond. And he wanted to bury Mother there in 1935. That would have been an enormous expense. Hollywood Cemetery opened in 1849 and is a large, sprawling cemetery of rolling hills and winding paths overlooking the James River. Two United States presidents are buried there, James Monroe and John Tyler, as well as the only Confederate States president, Jefferson Davis. Twenty-five Confederate generals are buried there as well, more than any other cemetery in the country. It's listed on the National Register of Historic Places and is actually a tourist attraction.

I don't know how Daddy managed the finances but he did it — he buried Mother there. And he took me with him.

As I said, at the time she died, we were up at the Island Inn for the summer, so the night before we left to catch the train, that's where we were. We had a safe at the house in which we kept silverware and things — more to protect them from fire than theft. They opened the safe and there was a letter in there apparently to Daddy from Mother. You could see Daddy was very upset when he opened it. I never heard him speak about it, though.

When we got to the cemetery, after the ceremony was over Daddy simply said, "She's gone," and of course he missed her and talked about her but those were the two most emotional periods.

Aunt Charlotta moved in with us to help Daddy after Mother died. She was devoted to Daddy, as he was to her. It was a lot for her to take on, and that's a huge understatement. The situation didn't last very long. Aunt Char got along with Uncle Ernest and with John, and she intended to stay. I wasn't there; Granny took me to school in September, the same day the 1935 hurricane came through. Seems to me I'm always managing to avoid hurricanes but I assure you it is not intentional.

Whatever her good intentions, for Aunt Char it was just an impossible situation. I'm sure Sam and John both were giving her the "You're not my mother" sort of thing. Daddy would have been trying to make peace. And Aunt Char was very set in her ways. It just didn't work out. This is supposition on my part; as I said, I wasn't there. But I believe it was a doomed situation before it started, with two

Aunt Charlotta

wild hyenas and a man working full-time trying to keep the thing going, plus an odd full-grown man in the household. Teenagers are sometimes the most stupid people in the world until they're parents themselves; then they grow up and are amazed at how much smarter their parents have gotten. For a time I had no use for my Granny and Aunt. I don't like to admit it now. But even after Aunt Char moved out, we had Christmas at her place every year instead of at home.

GOOD CHILDHOOD MEMORIES

Along with these sad memories, I also have many wonderful memories of my childhood on Sanibel. Those days are gone forever, not just for me and for the others lucky enough to have grown up on the island the way it was in those days, but gone forever for everyone now. I hate change more than anyone but I recognize we have to deal with it and adjust to it. Still, it's nice to

remember the past sometimes, and it's important to learn about what it was like before things changed. History is important. My brother Sam knew that very well as he worked so hard to help establish the Sanibel Historical Museum and Village.

I did have "nannies" when I was two, three, and four years old: Aunt Hattie and Arsenia. I can just remember they were there, but nothing else really. There's one picture of my nanny holding me up and it does not bring back any memories.

I had nannies when I was a very young child and the family could afford it, before the farming collapsed.

In fact, I have very little memory of any servants. There were part-time cooks to help Mother with the housekeeping. I remember one of them had a little dog named Flossie. That's about the extent of what I remember about her.

42

A woman named Ella Austin came every Monday to wash clothes. She boiled them in a cast iron cauldron and a day or two later she did the ironing. Her husband would drive her up in a big Lincoln or Cadillac, I don't remember which. Mother cooked most of the time.

Daddy was very successful during this time period. He had already accomplished a lot to make our home life more comfortable. He had put indoor plumbing in the house way back in 1908 when the windmill and water tank and guest room (the west wing) were built. And I know when my mother got back from the hospital after I was born in

Daddy holds me in the Palm Room at the Homestead.

1931, Daddy had put electricity in the house as a gift to her. It was produced by a small generator – 32 volts of DC current. Big cells made up the battery and had to be charged every day. The first generator was a Fairbanks-Morris and it was destroyed in the 1926 hurricane when it filled with saltwater. The second one was a small Delco. The opening was very small and stood about one foot high. It was full of acid and had plates down inside like the inside of a car battery but these were glass. The glass was the casing for the battery.

This was about 20 years before the whole island got electricity. Mostly our electricity was a cord hanging down from the ceiling.

Daddy's success took a beating, though, with the hurricane of 1926, which wiped out the entire store and every last bit of its inventory. That was quite a blow, and many of the luxuries we had, if you can call them that, were lost.

Some of the nicest things I remember have to do with holidays, as it is with all children I guess. On Easter mornings we would sometimes had a bunch of new little biddies. Those chicks were so cute. The chickens were very tame but they didn't come in the yard, they were away from the house. We'd feed them and walk around with them; sometimes you could just pick them up right off the roost.

At Easter time when I was growing up with Mother, we'd wake up in the morning and hidden inside the house would be these candy eggs that don't melt; they're kind of sickly sweet. After breakfast we went out in the yard and hunted for colored Easter eggs. I used

43

Daddy and his sons: John on his lap, me and Sam

to do that for my kids, too. The joy of finding an Easter egg even as I can remember now: whew, that was a thrill! The funny thing was sometimes you would be doing some work in the yard the following summer and you would find an egg. Not often, but occasionally.

Christmas was wonderful, and it didn't begin in our house until Christmas. It didn't start the Fourth of July like it does today; it started for the children on Christmas morning. And it lasted the 12 days of Christmas, until Epiphany. Today all the holidays are celebrated weeks or even months in advance. I don't like that.

Another great thing about Christmas was you got out of school. Mother would wrap presents to send to relatives and decorate the house — but there was no Christmas tree yet. On Christmas Eve we went to bed and hung up our stockings. Previously we'd sent a note to Santa, and we left cookies and milk. Miraculously the next morning there was a beautiful Christmas tree and two-thirds of the milk was gone. We believed Santa brought the tree. I continued that tradition with my family and my daughter Anne tells me she really appreciated that. My present wife June thinks the kids should put the tree up so they can enjoy taking part in it, and I can understand that point of view.

My mother always made sure we ate three hot meals a day consisting of a variety of vegetables (I was 35 years old before I even knew some people preferred to eat their vegetables half-cooked), fruit and meat; we always had fresh eggs. Christmas Day was no different as far as Mother was concerned. We had to eat our healthy breakfast and perform our chores before we were allowed to go in to the Christmas tree.

When Mother was alive, meals were big deals. We always had a big meal in the middle of the day on Sunday, usually baked chicken or turkey. Quite often we had the preacher there and fed him.

Some people ate sea turtles in those days but we didn't. I've heard the school bus driver would stop and pick up gophers, and that could be true, but not in my time. I never heard of a gopher tortoise until I was well into my adulthood. My favorite meal as a child was simply whatever food was on the table.

That was 80 years ago, and I still remember those Christmas traditions. We'd string popcorn and cranberries, alternating the two, for decoration. And we'd make garland out of different colored construction paper cut into strips using glue made of flour and water to make rings. We'd wake up in the morning and the stockings that had been on the mantle were by our beds with always an orange in the bottom and little silly toys and stuff like that.

After Mother died we celebrated Christmas at the Island Inn in Granny's cottage. In fact, we ate up there almost every Sunday, particularly during the off-season. They always had a cook, a black woman named Mariah. She could take this Florida beef that you couldn't cut with a hacksaw and make it into the most tender and delicious meal. There's probably a nostalgia factor at work here and if you gave it to me today it wouldn't taste the same as it tastes in my mind.

I believe in the famous editorial that appeared in *The Sun* in New York in 1897, *Yes, Virginia, there is a Santa Claus*. I say Santa Claus is more real than anything in the world — not a man with boots and all that of course, but what he represents: compassion for other people. I can't express it in words. It's something inside of you and in the air, but it's very real. I can't abide kids who just want to spoil it for the younger ones by telling them there's no Santa. There was Santa aplenty on Sanibel, let me tell you — this kind of Santa:

Eight-year-old Virginia O'Hanlon wrote a letter to the editor of New York's Sun, and the quick response was printed as an unsigned editorial September 21, 1897. The work of veteran newsman Francis Pharcellus Church has since become history's most reprinted newspaper editorial, appearing in part or whole in dozens of languages in books, movies, and other editorials, and on posters and stamps.

DEAR EDITOR: I am 8 years old. Some of my little friends say there is no Santa Claus. Papa says, "If you see it in The Sun, it's so." Please tell me the truth; is there a Santa Claus?
VIRGINIA O'HANLON, 115 West Ninety-Fifth Street

VIRGINIA, your little friends are wrong. They have been affected by the skepticism of a skeptical age. They do not believe except [what] they see. They think that nothing can be which is not comprehensible by their little minds. All minds, Virginia, whether they be men's or children's, are little. In this great universe of ours man is a mere insect, an ant, in his intellect, as compared with the boundless world about him, as measured by the intelligence capable of grasping the whole of truth and knowledge.

Yes, VIRGINIA, there is a Santa Claus. He exists as certainly as love and generosity and devotion exist, and you know that they abound and give to your life its highest beauty and joy. Alas! how dreary would be the world if there were no Santa Claus. It would be as dreary as if there were no VIRGINIAS. There would be no childlike faith then, no poetry, no romance to make tolerable this existence. We should have no enjoyment, except in sense and sight. The eternal light with which childhood fills the world would be extinguished.

Not believe in Santa Claus! You might as well not believe in fairies! You might get your papa to hire men to watch in all the chimneys on Christmas Eve to catch Santa Claus, but even if they did not see Santa Claus coming down, what would that prove? Nobody sees Santa Claus, but that is no sign that there is no Santa Claus. The most real things in the world are those that neither children nor men can see. Did you ever see fairies dancing on the lawn? Of course not, but that's no proof that they are not there. Nobody can conceive or imagine all the wonders there are unseen and unseeable in the world.

You may tear apart the baby's rattle and see what makes the noise inside, but there is a veil covering the unseen world which not the strongest man, nor even the united strength of all the strongest men that ever lived, could tear apart. Only faith, fancy, poetry, love, romance, can push aside that curtain and view and picture the supernal beauty and glory beyond. Is it all real? Ah, VIRGINIA, in all this world there is nothing else real and abiding.

My Granny Matthews

When I was growing up, Christmas was at the church. The school teacher lived on the island and we would have little plays. One time I had to go out on stage alone; my mother just insisted that I do it. I was in plays at school, but this one was at the Community Church on Christmas Eve. I was supposed to come out on stage all by myself and blow a horn and say something like, "The King is coming." And I was terrified. I don't remember how it came off. I was 12 or 13.

I was home every Christmas from college and prep school. After Mother died we would go up to Aunt Char's and Granny's cottage and open presents and have Christmas dinner up there. The hotel was open and running but we had our Christmas in Granny's cottage. Then we would go out on the beach and play touch football in the afternoon.

All my life I was on Sanibel for all but two Christmases, the two I was in the Army. I didn't like being away, and I probably did about the same thing on those Christmas Days as I did any other day.

In Truax Field in Madison, Wisconsin, for some cockeyed reason I decided to go into town on Christmas night – alone. The Army buses inside the camp stopped running at midnight or so, and I got there late. City buses stopped at the gate and I had to walk to my squadron. I got so cold – I don't think I've ever been so cold – I couldn't feel my chin. Snow was all over the ground. I stopped at every orderly room I could to warm up. I was always moaning and groaning about the cold weather but a bunch of the others got frostbitten ears and noses and I didn't.

The other Christmas I was in the Army in Salt Lake City and one of my buddies and I tried to go to church. Of course we didn't get there very early and we couldn't get in. The yard was full as well as the building.

Those were the only two white Christmases I ever experienced, in Wisconsin and in Utah.

One Christmas Eve Daddy, Uncle Ernest and Robert Cockerill dressed up like the "Three Kings of Orient Are." Daddy never remembered any of the words. It was hilarious. That would be partly because of Daddy's poor eyesight – he couldn't read the music or the songs or the words. They were dressed up in real full trousers almost like pantaloons. That was some threesome. Sam and John loved to talk about that.

> **One Christmas Eve Daddy, Uncle Ernest and Robert Cockerill dressed up like the "Three Kings of Orient Are."**

Daddy sometimes conducted the services, always out of the Episcopalian prayer book, but he never gave any sermons. Then the congregation would break up and the kids would go to one group and adults to another and sing hymns.

Santa Claus always came and every child on the island got a present. Even if you had just come in the night before, we had something for you. If we didn't have a child's name, we'd ask about "an 18-month-old girl" so we could get her name and Santa would be able to call it out. We always tried to call out the child's name ; it was a homey tradition. I remember when I got a little older, I felt a little embarrassed sometimes, thinking why was I getting a present?

The Community House

After a while this tradition became difficult to sustain because we had so many children and there were more young people on the island. I don't know how the gifts were paid for – whether it was the church, or someone collected money from all of us. Eventually the gathering got too big for the church so we moved it to the Community House. Then it got too big for the Community House and we had to give it up. After Daddy died, that sort of thing died down.

One or two years after Daddy died, Priscilla Murphy came to me and wanted to know if I would conduct some meetings like Daddy did until we got a minister over here. They were held at the Sanibel Community Church which was non-sectarian. Uncle Ernest was one of the original trustees who built the Sanibel Community Church, which was to be a Methodist Church although Uncle Ernest was Episcopalian. I would read the Christmas story from St. Luke, say some prayers, we would sing, and other things. If a minister happened to be here, he would conduct these services.

A regular minister was something of a luxury, though. In the winter we might have a minister, the reason being that the winter people had money to pay the preacher.

Not all my childhood memories are of holidays, though. When we were 10 or 11 years old or younger, we loved mangoes. In the summer at the Island Inn, Daddy would spread newspapers out and we would take all our clothes off to eat them because mangoes are so juicy. The mangoes were only available in the summer, but you appreciate things more when you haven't had them for a while. Daddy would peel them and after we ate them, we would run down to the beach and get into the water to wash off. It didn't matter that we were in our birthday suits because there wasn't anybody around.

One time I saw a little girl — 2½ years old if she was that old — and people got upset because she was running around in her birthday suit. How ridiculous! Of course, these days they almost are naked and wearing clothes no bigger than three postage stamps. In Mother's time only your ankles could show.

Later in life after we'd grown up and we'd get hot or just wanted to go swimming, we'd simply hang our clothes on a piece of driftwood or something and go swimming. It wasn't being daring or anything, there just wasn't anybody around and you knew there wasn't going to be anybody around. From The Gables west, there was nothing and that's where we would do it. Between Casa Ybel and the lighthouse, there was nobody. Elsewhere an occasional car would go by. An occasional car – that's the way it is when you're raised in the country, which Sanibel certainly was. Every time a car went by, you looked to see who was in it and waved, because there just weren't that many cars (and hardly any containing people you didn't know). When I was growing up, two or three cars on the road in one mile was a traffic jam. At school, when an airplane went over, the teacher would let us out of school so we could look at it. I can guarantee not a single solitary soul had ever been in an airplane — probably never been near an airplane.

Back then, there were plenty of places on the island where you could be sure of being alone.

The only time we took a risk, Sam and I were on the bay side by the store and the lighthouse, something to do with some work. We got real hot, looked around, and there was a boat with two men on it and no other boaters anywhere to be seen. We stripped down to the buff and got in the water. Well, here comes the boat of course. We didn't think anything of it, though — so what, a boat with two men; they don't give a doggone. Then here was this woman on the boat after all, with a hat pulled down way over her head, in a man's shirt – even up close you'd think she was a man. I don't remember the woman reacting at all but her husband got ... fussy. That was the only time we had any problem.

A quiet road on Sanibel

Years later, eccentric people who called themselves "naturalists" were going to Bowman's Beach in the nude. A woman named Alice Kylo found out and the story was she threw tacks in the road and came out with her shotgun filled with rock salt besides. Her husband was a really nice guy who worked in the post office and adopted a little Oriental boy. She was a busybody, though — always in everybody's business.

GOING TO SCHOOL ON THE ISLAND

I'm in the middle row, third from the right. John is kneeling at the far left. Also shown are Preston Woodring, George Henning, Mrs. Bahaus, Sherwin Mayer and Gertrude Henning.

I first started formal school when I was about seven years old, in second grade. Mother taught me kindergarten and first grade at home using the Calvert School curriculum from Baltimore, Maryland. She was strict with schoolwork; there was no getting out of work with Mother, no fiddling around except maybe when Uncle Clark, her brother, came around. You did your work or else. I probably learned as much with Mother as I learned later on in school. But we had plenty of play time, too, which is important. Up to the 8th grade, I didn't do a lick of homework, didn't even know what that word was. It just wasn't done.

I went to the one-room Sanibel School on Periwinkle Way in second grade with Mrs. Wiles. The school was located just east of where Tahitian Gardens is today. There were

Above: The school as the Playhouse Theatre
Right: The school at the Historical Village today, restored as closely as possible to the original.

50

open fields all around the school. Some will remember it as the old Pirate Playhouse, which it was before it was moved to the Historical Museum & Village and restored as closely as possible to the way it looked in the time I was a student there. Moving that school was a big accomplishment of Sam's and all the other people who made it happen.

I don't remember much about school when I started. It was just one room and there was a library with about a dozen books in it, so maybe we should call it a "book room" instead of a library. The boys and girls lined up on opposite sides of the steps and said the Pledge of Allegiance before going in to class. There was one room, one school, one door, one cabinet, one pencil sharpener, but two 2-hole outhouses. Today, they have a piano in the schoolhouse in the museum, but there was no piano! I know, because the Community House and the church shared one, and I hauled it on a pickup truck between the two about a million times when we used to have dances later on.

Being out in the boonies, only occasionally did we have a music teacher who would come around. We used to have plays then, especially at Christmastime.

It must have been hard on a teacher to have all the grades in one room, but I think in some cases it was the younger children who got the advantage of it. There was a maximum of 31 to 33 children at one time, first through eighth grade. I remember the older students would listen to the younger children read. We had to practice writing. I don't know what they did about arithmetic except I remember reciting the times tables. We had spelling contests, and I remember studying geography, capitals, and cities. Students who graduate from high school today have no idea where Washington, DC is, so I guess we did okay.

School was different in those days. I have a copy of a school exam from 1895. It was an 8th grade exam but I'll wager students today couldn't answer the questions that were on that test. The only thing they teach now in a lot of schools is how not to bring knives and guns.

I went to an academically challenging prep school, though, and I didn't have any real problem with the work there, so the Sanibel School must have done a good job. It's amazing how those teachers taught us, especially considering how they used to have to break up fights all the time. Every time we had a PTA meeting, they had to stop to break up the fights. That really upset Mother.

Some of the things we did you'd probably end up in jail for today. I think of the fights with classmates Preston Woodring and James Stuart – but then five minutes later it was forgotten and we were friends again.

During our half-hour recess we played games like tag, Red Rover, Annie Over, and pickup sticks. Later on we had softball but we called it baseball — even though by that time the ball really was soft, all worn out and almost egg shaped. "Softball" is one of the biggest misnomers I ever heard anyway. Those balls are hard! I know; I've been hit by them.

Sam, me and John

By our rules, if you knocked the ball over the fence you were out and the game was over because you had to go get the ball in the saw grass. First base was the fence post, second base was some bars or something, and I don't remember if we even had a third base or what home plate was.

Later on we went outside the school grounds and played out there where we had a little more room. One time we had a slide that came from the school board. The way we'd speed ourselves up was to use bread wrappers, which in those days had wax on them. The slide would get pretty hot so you would take that bread wrapper and the wax on it would slick it up so you would go faster. Of course there was always some little kid who was terrified. I was probably one of them to start with.

I remember one girl in particular, Dorothy Price, who was a winter person. Her mother started the 'Tween Waters Inn. She had a chicken farm in Bristol Virginia/Tennessee (the state line runs right down Main Street). Her father wasn't too successful, I don't think, and she was the lone daughter. But the reason I'm writing about her is that she used to come to school with shorts on and that was quite intriguing to the boys. I also remember another girl who sat in front of me and she had long hair that she kept flipping onto my desk and it was so annoying. So all these years later, I remember what was intriguing and what was annoying.

We sure played a lot of games, boys and girls both. Of course there was hide-and-go-seek and tag, but maybe someone will remember some of these:

In Annie Over, kids were on both sides of the school house at the same time and would call out "Annie Over" and throw the ball over the roof. If somebody on the other side got it, they could run around and try to tag the person so you could bring them over to your side and increase your chances of winning. It never even occurred to us that anybody would cheat.

We played a game called Stealing Sticks where you'd draw a line and put six sticks in a circle in the back, then stand back so many feet from the line. The object was to get over to the sticks before somebody tagged you; if you made it, you could steal one. Once you got your hand on a stick, you got a free ride.

Red Rover might be a little more well-known. You had a team and you had to hold hands. The girls always played this one, too — we didn't know any difference in those days, we were all just children. You said, "Red Rover, Red Rover, let Francis come over," or some other child's name. You had to look at the other team and see where you could break into the line. If you succeeded, you could choose a person to take back to your team. The object was to deplete the other side.

Every once in a while we got real bad and went and got a long pole. Then when the girls would go in the outhouse, we'd put the pole under there and rock the outhouse. Naturally, to say we'd catch a little hell for doing that sort of thing is an understatement. That was not an everyday occurrence, but it happened. Apparently as a youngster I had a reputation of being a Dennis the Menace type, as did the other two Bailey boys. I have absolutely no idea why. When you don't have a lot of high-powered toys like kids do today, you find ways to occupy yourself that may not please everybody!

> **Naturally, to say we'd catch a little hell for doing that sort of thing is an understatement.**

We also played Cowboys and Indians. I don't think the girls played this game as much as the boys, but they played everything else. It was not a very well structured game to say the least. Our pistols were pretty much just sticks carved out of cypress shingles in the general shape of a gun. Cypress shingles are very thin, so it was easy to do. But they looked like sticks, not much like pistols. It seems so silly now. We just pointed our pistols and said, "Bang, bang, dead man!" and the guy would get up instantly and say, "New man!" There weren't that many kids, so it was kind of necessary. The fun of it was really a matter of running all the time and hiding behind things, I think. There had to be some limitations to the game but I swear I don't remember them.

I remember this: We played hard. I never broke any bones, though, except for some ribs and that was fairly recently. When I broke my ribs, the pain was so bad I was glad I never broke anything before. In the old days, if you ran, stumbled, or fell, you got up and kept going.

I miss those school days, even though Mother was strict about them. The only way we got out of school was to actually go to a doctor. (And islanders did get sick. When the winter people came down, they brought diseases: measles, whooping cough, chicken pox. That still happens today. You have to be careful when they start coming in.) We got punished if we didn't toe the line. For example, Mother loved baseball but we couldn't go with her to games if we had to miss school.

School started at 8:30 in the morning and went to 3 o'clock in the afternoon with a half hour for recess and one hour for lunch. We went home for lunch. As I've said, Mother was very careful about how we ate. We only lived a mile from school. If our folks had to go into town for some reason, we would eat at school. We were probably the only ones who did go home. One day a Mr. Jenkins took us home for lunch – it was like a picnic when we had lunch out – and we had pancakes for lunch. I had never had pancakes for lunch! Of course, we always were most interested in eating as fast as we could so we could get back to playing.

For the first few years of school, we Baileys were the only children on the east side of the island. There were winter people at Chadwick's, which is South Seas today. There was Preston Woodring down in the swamp, but you had to get there by boat or by climbing through the swamp. In later years, the school bus did come down near our home after the Palmers got here and lived at the lighthouse. There was room in the bus, so they'd stop and pick us up. In those days things were pretty free and easy.

I got to climb the lighthouse once because I happened to be down there playing with the Palmers. They weren't as restrictive about those things then – the Palmer kids used to play in there. The view is nice from the lighthouse, but I've been up a few times in a helicopter, and I have to say that's really nice, that's the best. Things are so prohibitive today, it's a shame – we never would be allowed in the lighthouse now. Back then we had a lot of liberty, and we never locked anything on the island, either, except we did lock the store. We would go to church on Sunday, lock the front door and leave the back door open.

Mother had us take dancing lessons too, but we hated that dancing stuff. Robert Cockerill, the one who was a member of the Three Kings of Orient Are performance) was a retired British Army officer from India. He and his wife Lilias built their own house at the end of Main Street. She would try to teach us dancing while her husband played the piano. He couldn't play one note without having four pieces of music in front of him. So she would clap her hands and stomp her feet and yell, "Robert, Robert, Robert." Oh, we hated it! Maybe the girls enjoyed it, I don't know. Mother made us do it, maybe to build grace. And there wasn't much else going on, you know. It was some activity for us other than digging ditches. We did it for maybe two or three years. Even in the 1930s, we had dances at the Sanibel Community House.

I did enjoy dancing, primarily square dancing, later in my life after the war in the 1950s and '60s at the Community House. Of course there was no air conditioning and literally every stitch of clothing you had on would be wet. The only place with air conditioning when I was growing up was the movie theater. Down here – well, even up north – you're in air conditioning all the time, down to 70 degrees and sometimes even colder than that. Then you go outside and it's in the 90s, and then you maybe exert yourself, and it makes a difference, the sudden change. I don't think it's healthy.

The Community House was important to island life in many ways.

In spite of the heat, we just went at that square dancing whole hog. I used to like to square dance with Goldie and Alan Nave. There also were the Jacks, Gaults, Stahlins, and McQuades. I still remember some of the calls, or parts of them. There were plays at the Community House and the school, too, and on Christmas Eve at the church with the children and some of the adults.

MY BROTHERS WERE MY PLAYMATES

I always say two-thirds of the Sanibel School graduating class of 1935 is still on the island – but there were only three of us to start with! Preston Woodring was in the same grade as I but he was older; he's gone now. Preston was brother to Ralph Woodring who owns The Bait Shop on Periwinkle Way. Preston went straight into the

Ralph Woodring with me in 2012

Coast Guard after high school. Then WW II came along and he made a career of it. Preston lived at Woodring Point and you could only get there by boat. Because of that, we had very little to do with him other than at school, just as a matter of practicality. A family, the Gordons, lived at the corner where Bank of the Islands is now, Periwinkle Way and Casa Ybel. They had a lot of girls and in those days, I wouldn't have anything to do with girls! They had one boy, Frank, who ended up in reform school.

Later on there were the Palmer kids at the lighthouse, but William was the only one to play with. There was the Wiles family, but the older brother Homer didn't live on the island. Homer's daughter Barbara, who was a little older (her aunt and uncle were Clarence and Ruth Rutland), used to come over and play hide-and-seek once or twice a year. The older generation of Wiles consisted of widower "TM," who kept such a clean house, Sam always said you could eat off the floors.

Sam and our first cousin Matt Clapp used to fish and claim they'd found fishing holes. I was never much of a fisherman. In fact, I don't know what a fishing hole is. To me, it seemed like fishing consisted of drinking beer and moving the boat around. Nobody ever caught anything.

The first time I ever heard of red tide was when I was away at school. One time coming home for Christmas vacation, the dead fish in San Carlos Bay were

Boys and nanny in the sandbox.

unbelievable. We had some cold weather that killed the fish but I don't remember any red tide. I'm not saying there wasn't any; after all, the Baileys weren't seafarers. Although I did catch two fish one time and the run boat man gave me a nickel for them.

It's only logical, really, that it was almost always my brothers and I doing things together. It was about five miles to the lighthouse. The next closest family was the Stewarts up past the American Legion, 300 or 400 yards

John and Sam with me lifting the wheelbarrow

past the curve. From the end of Sanibel to the north end of Captiva, if anybody had a car, it was one car, and we didn't get to Captiva very often. In those days, Captiva was a million miles away. If you got there once every two years, it was a lot.

There just was nobody around back then. There were two little colored kids, grandsons of Peter Burns. We played with them, but not that much. When night time came they went their way and we went ours. That's just the way it was.

We thought the world of Peter Burns, my brothers and I did. He was a geechee from South Carolina (geechee is a term used to refer to the direct descendants of African slaves who settled in the South Carolina low country and speak patois or Creole languages) and had maybe one or two teeth. Between speaking geechee and having no teeth, most people couldn't understand him, but we got so we could understand him. He was an alcoholic,

My brother John

unfortunately, and that caused his demise. He worked for Daddy, and Daddy never paid him with money –he gave him food. And Peter would come in with catalogs with the clothes picked out that he needed and Daddy would get them for him. But if you gave him any money it went to whiskey. Some people made the mistake of doing that.

So my playmates were my brothers. Most of the time we got along pretty good. We just took each other as we came. We would get mad sometimes and not like each other, like kids do: "You got more than I got." And then we would get over it. In later life, John used to complain to me that Sam and I were stronger and healthier than he was. But John had done some things I would never do as far as cowboying.

John had a good memory. He was unwell as a youngster. They said he had heart trouble but I don't know about that. He would lie in bed for a year, maybe two. They wouldn't even let him brush his teeth. I picked him up out of bed once to take him out to the porch and it was just like picking up a little doll. I guess it passed, though. He ran cross-country and rodeo in college and that takes a good heart. Right up to the end of his life, he was doing calf roping. We used to kid him and say he was in five different graduating classes in Fort Myers High School because being sick set him back; actually I think it was only three. He didn't finish college. He was one year behind me until five or six years after I got out. I came back December 1948, and John graduated in March 1949. Everyone went up to Gainesville for the ceremony. I think we took my first wife Pauline with us, before we were married. Sam was there, too.

Sam and I went out carousing all night after the thing. We had it all figured out: Sam was going to drive the car. Daddy didn't want to drive and I was hung over. Daddy announced when we got in the car that I was going to drive. That ended the discussion: headache or not, I drove the car. I think Daddy was telling us we shouldn't have been carousing and trying to teach us about consequences. He taught us a lot of things by his actions instead of with words.

The Koreshan Unity where John and I delivered coconut trees.

John and I did a lot of things together. Whenever he was home, we would play softball, until he married in 1950. Daddy used to sell coconut trees to the Koreshans in Estero, and John and I used to take them down there and come back in the morning. We used to stay in all kinds of places. One night we stayed in the guard gatehouse at Page Field right on the cement floor with a baseball glove for our pillow. We had to sleep in there to get out of the mosquitoes.

We used to play Monopoly like crazy: Sam and Matt Clapp, our first cousin, versus John and me – and Sam and Matt were not above a little sleight of hand. And Sam and

John used to go camping in the Everglades. They'd take frying pans, some bacon, and guns. I am not a camper and Daddy wasn't either. Daddy would say he could never be too comfortable. But if hardship was necessary, he endured it; that didn't bother him.

John and I got ourselves into some messes. There was no causeway yet of course, and no cars for us kids. We used to go to Fort Myers to play ball. Sometimes we would take the last ferry over there and bum a ride into town. One time in about 1946, though, we got the bright idea to go to Fort Myers Beach and catch a bus they had there. John had a homemade boat and a little 7½ horsepower motor he got second or third hand. It was always breaking down. This time it was running perfectly and that irked John. He took it apart to find out what was "wrong" with it – then he couldn't get it back together. John said it was running good and he had to find out why. There was a strong tide and we rowed that homemade boat hard and heavy. Daddy wasn't worried about us because we weren't supposed to be coming back but spending the night over there. Some kind person came by and towed us in that day. Needless to say I had some choice words to say to my brother. It took quite a while for those blisters to heal. That darn motor's still up in John's barn in Jacksonville.

It makes me think of all the things you have to do when you get older that seem like a trial or require so much planning but back in your youth you just got up and did them. You didn't worry about where you had to sleep until it was time to go to sleep – then you worried about it. Of course you could get a room in a hotel for $2 or $3 – if you had it; that was a lot of money then.

One time Daddy and Mother were away for the evening and Aunt Char was taking care of us. Sam and I were having problems with our little generator that charged the batteries for the lights. We thought we knew how to work it. The starter wouldn't work but we got a big old heavy crank. The crank hit Sam in the head. We had been missing and Aunt Char was looking for us. Sam said, "Do you think she'll know we've been out here?" With blood streaming down his face! For a long time, though, I was not required to do any house maintenance work. Later when I was grown I had to stain the house with creosote.

Then there was the time we picked up people from everywhere to make a team and play a softball game on Cayo Costa. The field was full of gopher holes and small sea grasses. The other team was supposed to have this great pitcher –

Cayo Costa — not the best terrain for softball

we played fast-pitch softball. And Sam was supposed to be a hotshot hitter. Supposedly there was a big duel between them. I don't remember who won the game but that wasn't important. The important thing was just to have fun. There was certainly a lot of hype leading up to it. We didn't have many games like that, though. Gopher holes have a tendency to slow you down.

Me with my daughter, Mary Mead

We still were doing some crazy things many years later. Sam, John and I were all in Spain on an Associated Grocers trip. I think it coincided with my daughter Mary Mead's graduation. We went to some bull ring someplace and they had young little bulls. Then they brought out some donkeys and a bottle of champagne – if you could ride the donkey and pick up the champagne, you could have it. We were all feeling a little good on sangria, but Sam and I knew we couldn't do it. We knew John could do it, though. We finally convinced him to try it and sure enough, he did it. He kept that bottle of champagne for two years before he ever opened it, maybe longer.

We always got along, Sam and I. Like all brothers, we had our fights. We got along particularly when we were younger. When we got older we weren't together that much. In 1946 both Sam and John were here for a while and we played ball together — John and I were on a County Championship softball team. Later, John lived in several places doing seven-days-a-week jobs. My job was seven days a week, too. We used to go to Tampa for some of Sam's games when we could.

I BECOME A BEEKEEPER

I worked for Daddy in the summers, but only when I couldn't get out of it! I used to like to take a wheel of cheese in the store and slice off a real thin piece and eat it. We carried fish-shaped lollipop suckers that I liked, too. They cost two cents and they were big. We had no baked goods, though, because everybody made their own.

Before long, I found something I was interested in that occupied a lot of my time.

I spent more than 20 years working with bees.

From the time I was 13 or 14 years old right up until 1952, I spent three or four days a week working with bees. I had to take the honey off, extract it, and put the combs back in. It takes time, but I enjoyed it. My father did an awful lot of the work as well, especially when I was in the Army. I worked at the store here and there, too. Daddy always had a garden, so I also worked in the garden. At one point Daddy had a garden across the road and we had to haul water over there one pail at a time. I did not enjoy that.

The bee business started this way. Right after Christmas 1935, Howard Passage, a shop teacher in Bloomingdale, Michigan, came to Sanibel. I don't know how he ended up on Sanibel; he just showed up. Daddy was always befriending people. Mr. Passage was in a trailer with a whole bunch of beehives, 10 or 12 of them. There was a building across the street from the old packing house but at first, Mr. Passage parked his trailer in our yard. After a while Mother decided that wasn't the thing to do, so then he parked across the street. Sometime later we all went over; Sam was a little young but didn't want anything to do with bees anyway. I just became interested. Mr. Passage talked to me and we made an agreement: I would get half the honey and half of the increase in the hives for taking care of the bees.

There are several ways to increase the hives. You can buy queen bees or let them form. Bees naturally swarm but you don't want them to do that. Bees will take an egg and build a queen cell; then they feed the queen royal jelly. In fact, they'll make several queens. But if you leave the hive alone and the queen hatches out, she'll destroy the other ones.

I started working with Mr. Passage and he taught me. Everything I learned was either from him or from reading a book, The ABC & XYZ of Bee Culture, by Amos Ives Root. I was here during most of the honey flow but there's not a whole lot you do with them during the winter time, even down here.

In those days, we had orange blossom honey, but that didn't last very long; we had wildflower, mangrove, and palmetto honey. Apparently Brazilian pepper makes honey, too, but we didn't have more than three or four Brazilian pepper trees on the island. That's hard to believe, isn't it? We had one on our property, and people would come to get boughs to decorate for Christmas.

We sold some of the honey in the store, but the bulk of it we sold in 55-gallon drums to the baker in Fort Myers, Alexander Bakery.

I have been stung on every square inch of my body from the bottom of my feet to the top of my head. But I survived. Kids today are never exposed to anything. They're shot so full of antibiotics that if they ever catch anything, it kills them – maybe not literally; I'm exaggerating to make a point. I've heard the venom that comes from a bee sting is ounce for ounce many times stronger than what comes out of a rattlesnake. I don't know if that's true but I did read that in the U.S., bee stings cause three to four times more deaths than do venomous snakebites.

Obviously I didn't keep the bees while I was in the Army. I worked with the bees until a little after Daddy passed away in 1952. Then I decided I had too much work that needed to be tended to.

A MORE NATURAL ISLAND THAN TODAY

The island looked very different when I was young. There was very little tall vegetation. When people first got here I don't think there were any coconut palms. None of the pictures I've ever seen had any. In the early 1940s, there were just miles with no interference by man except the road.

Way back, wire grass grew in clumps, and farmers would plant their seeds in between the clumps. Wire grass was about as thick around as the lead in a pencil. After a while the farmers would dig it up and plow the land. Now you wouldn't do much plowing anymore. Things change and over time, almost every inch of arable land had been stirred up to farm.

We're living now with the result of introducing those farm seeds, which bring birds — which is the way nature wants it. We've also imported exotics like Australian pines (which can be kept under control), Brazilian pepper, melaleuca, and bottlebrush. That was thought of as a savior because it was going to dry up the Everglades. It just changed many things. We have learned a lot since then. Before people knew better, though, they thought the

Captiva Road lined with beautiful Australian pines

Everglades was a swamp with no value. Now we have learned it has value. If we get rid of it all, we will be jeopardizing our own lives and lifestyles and livelihoods. But even right-thinking people in those days thought it was a good thing to get rid of "the swamp"; they associated it with yellow fever and disease.

There's a story there was supposed to be treasure buried on Sanibel. I remember Daddy telling me many times people had dug holes looking for pirate treasure. Of course if those guys digging up the place had run across a shard, it would be nothing to them, whereas to an archeologist, it would have been treasure. People would dig holes and couldn't find anything. I do remember one Sunday people found something they thought was a midden (a shell mound from a human settlement.) A whole bunch of guys dug a hole you could put my office in but they didn't find a thing, not even bones. I don't think there were very many shell mounds on this island. Even so, not much thought was given to preserving the past and protecting the natural systems. People did what they thought was necessary to survive and to make life better for their families.

For example, the Caloosahatchee was connected to Lake Okeechobee because people thought it was great to use the rivers as canals, and we have had to fight the disastrous results of that on the island. We still have to. Even if we're able to succeed, it will take decades to fix the damage that has caused.

The Nave house which later housed Goumas Chocolates and now Nanny's Children's Clothing on Periwinkle Way west of the Community House.

A good many of the houses on Sanibel weren't painted. The reason was simple: paint costs money. Sometimes a builder would build the shell and frame and the owner could go in and finish it off, but at least you had a roof over your head and a floor underneath you in the meantime.

Another difference in the way Sanibel looked was the Australian pines. Daddy planted a lot of those pine trees along Periwinkle Way just for the beauty of them. Some people think they were planted to slow down erosion, but that's not the case at all.

A group of pine trees still stands today just to the right as you go into the original driveway of the homestead, and I'll tell you why they're there. When you have young plants and you're working hard all day to finish your chores, then at the end of the day you still haven't planted them all, you do what's called "heeling them up." You dig a shallow ditch, just scratch it out with a hoe or a shovel, and you temporarily put the plants in that shallow ditch until you can get back to planting them the next day. It was before I was born that someone did that in that location and never got back around to planting them. So they stayed there and grew in a clump. As you turn into the driveway, a short distance on the right-hand side is a cluster of Australian pines, the result of my father and his hands not getting back to the trees to plant them all those years ago. I'm quite sure my brothers and I have done the same thing since.

A cluster of Australian pines on the Homestead drive — grouped like this because the saplings were left to be planted the next day and no one ever got around to it.

I was sorry to see so many of the pines go. It was just short of being a criminal offense, what they did to those pine trees. And they killed more native vegetation cutting them down than Hurricane Charley did. But it's done, it's done. And now, if you had never seen it with the pine trees, Periwinkle Way looks very good, but I don't think the vegetation they planted really contributed to that. It's just stuff that grew.

Even during the daytime you would become mesmerized under the canopy that used to be on Periwinkle Way. After so many trees were gone from the island, I would have no idea where I was sometimes. Being country folk, my sense of direction is not by street signs, it's by oak trees and such. In Fort Myers, it's by buildings. Country folks do that: Where is Mr. Jones' house? Well, you go down and when you see the red cow turn left, then when you come to a big tree, turn right ... But what if the cow moves?

There are trees on this island I can't identify and that I don't think are native. I don't know what they are – maybe they're native but I never saw them when I was growing up. I know I never saw a blanket flower in all my life until quite recently. How can it be native when it hasn't been here for 100 years? Just like people are getting taller and bigger and healthier, it's the same thing with plants. Orange trees aren't native here, certainly, although key limes are. And I've wondered how you can possibly know something's going to be invasive until you've had them in the ground for a while. A lot of trees we have, people say aren't native, like guava, but I question that.

Sam and I used to have to pull weeds for Mother and were paid one cent for 10 weeds. Well, that was just too much work, so we took our toy wagons way in the back of the property, past the windmill, and loaded them up with peppers and told Mother we were weeding the path. That went over like a lead balloon. Forget that saying that you can fool all of the people some of the time, and some of the people all of the time. You couldn't fool Mother any of the time.

I had to pull weeds as a child. Farming was a big part of my life.

The bulk of the island was a farming community, but it wasn't 100 percent farming. There's practically nothing in life that is 100 percent. There were also boarding houses that evolved into hotels, and of course there was some fishing and fishing guides. With the tide turning and the evolution in transportation, the place soon became almost strictly a tourist destination. I've analyzed that aspect of the island and decided just about everybody here needs the tourists: the yard man needs tourists, the grocery store needs tourists, but Sammy Woodring, Ralph's brother and a commercial fisherman, really didn't. Sammy really knew these waters around here – he had to, to go up in these creeks and bayous. That's what we considered the Sanibel River to be, by the way – a bayou. That's all we ever called it.

Esperanza and Sam Woodring

Sam Woodring was married to Esperanza, and they were Ralph's parents. In addition to owning The Bait Box on Periwinkle Way, Ralph formed START, Solutions to Avoid Red Tide. Esperanza was born on Cayo Costa but her family lived north of St. Petersburg. Sammy was a child of Sam's by another wife and was a bootlegger. They're an interesting family, wonderful people and very important to the history of Sanibel.

Here's an example of how interesting they are; this happened in the mid 1990s. Ralph had two beautiful golden retrievers and someone stole one. The police found the dog but steadfastly refused to tell Ralph who took the dog — and for good reason. They

Their son Ralph

knew Ralph would have gone there and beaten the hell out of them. Someone stole a boat from him once and Ralph was shooting at him — he never hit him. I never found out who stole the dog; the police certainly weren't going to tell me.

Esperanza was a wonderful friend to our family.

Esperanza was a great person and a wonderful friend of our family. She did a lot of babysitting and helped me tremendously after my first wife Pauline died. Her eldest son Preston and I went to school together. We were in the same grade and when we weren't fighting, we were great friends.

Esperanza didn't necessarily have a big circle – by that I mean that while she had a great many friends, her world wasn't very large, living out at Woodring Point. She was also a guide and a very good fisherman. She could throw a cast net just about better than anybody. After her husband Sam

Esperanza casting a net

66

died, people would want to go fishing with Esperanza. I don't think she did much commercial fishing.

There were whiskey stills around on the island. The most recent still I remember is around 1949 or so. My aunt knew something was going on behind the Island Inn; she kept hearing this noise back there at night — a tapping and a tapping — and she couldn't figure out what it was. In addition, a man kept buying five pounds of sugar and a funnel, and she was getting suspicious and asked Daddy to look into it. Sure enough, in the back of the Island Inn the guy had a still. He was a friend of one of the Rhodes boys' father Henry, and the still was behind the servants' quarters. It was Henry's brother and he was a very simple-minded soul who had come to work for Aunt Char. She got Daddy to go up there, not only because he was her brother-in-law but because he was the law on the island, too. And sure enough, they found the still. Aunt Char had tried to get him to go off the island but he was so simple-minded that he wouldn't listen. And they caught him with this still right under her nose. It wasn't the making of the whiskey but the selling of it that was illegal. I don't remember any law enforcement surrounding that event. Sam said he drank some of that white lightning. I don't think I have ever tasted it.

As far as law enforcement on Sanibel, I'm not sure we really had any. Daddy was Justice of the Peace but I don't think he had any arresting power. When somebody got killed in an auto accident, though, he was there. One black woman got in a fight with another over a man and stabbed and killed her; Daddy was there.

There were pretty friendly fights every once in a while. I remember one time a guy split his friend's head open with an axe; that was a considered a friendly argument back then.

Much later we had a big fuss with the county. We said we didn't need to pay taxes to the Sheriff's department because we had our own police force. The county sheriff said he was a constitutional officer and he had to do it. We didn't get very far with our argument.

By 1966 half the island were deputy sheriffs, or at least it seemed that way. I used to say I was the only person on the island who wasn't either a deputy sheriff or a real estate agent.

Still, I used to make the store deposits at night and everyone wanted me to carry a pistol. They took me up to Bowman's Beach to practice and although I passed my

Daddy acted as law enforcement on the island.

marksmanship in the Army I didn't do very well. Finally I told them to take it away.

Totch Brown, famous for his escapades in the Everglades

Other places had a lot more trouble with crime than we did. Totch Brown was a big drug runner in the Everglades. He was running alcohol in the 1930s during Prohibition and later marijuana. He knew the waters down there. Down in the Ten Thousand Islands off the coast of Everglades City south of Marco Island, if you didn't know where you were going, you could get completely lost. Revenuers from Washington, the IRS men who went after bootleggers, would come down and in 10 minutes the bootleggers would completely lose them.

Drug running became sort of the thing to do. They didn't realize exactly the implications drug running has on other people. They would tell themselves, "Everybody else is doing it," so they'd think, "Why shouldn't I be doing it, I'll have some money?" Full bales of marijuana washed up on Sanibel beaches once, sometime after 1974. I never saw any of it — too busy, I reckon.

The Everglades Rod and Gun Club was quite a place and originally the railroad ran down there and it was the Collier County seat. I can remember when they moved it up to Naples.

The events in Peter Matthiessen's book, *Killing Mr. Watson*, happened years before I was born, around 1910, I think. According to legend, Edgar Watson was supposed to have killed the so-called Queen of the Outlaws, Belle Starr, back out West, as well as his field hands so that he didn't have to pay them, along with

The Everglades Rod and Gun Club

dozens of other people. He was married to a woman who was from a prominent family in Fort Myers. It was very isolated where he lived. Chocoloskee was nowhere. Ted Smallwood had a store that's still there as kind of a museum/gift shop. It made sense where he had his store — water was the mode of transportation. Likewise in the case of Sanibel Woodring Point was completely cut off except by boat traffic when I was growing up. They had to use little one-cylinder motors that went putt-putt-putt. Of course it gradually changed over the years.

REAL GROWTH BEGINS

Developers were digging canals before the causeway came; that's what Hugo Lindgren wanted. I remember I was at a meeting with some developer and afterwards the other people at the meeting said they thought I was going to jump up and fight the guy. I don't even like the word "developer."

In fact, Beachview Golf Club would be a municipal course today if not for Lindgren. John Kontinos, a developer, was working on Beachview and had to give Lindgren an answer on the loan by a certain time. Kontinos couldn't meet the deadline. He was close, but old moneybags cut him off, and now it's private.

The Butterknife community off of West Gulf Drive used to be an air strip; before that it was a sisal hemp field planted under President Franklin Roosevelt's program during the Depression. The airstrip was closed 20 years ago, give or take. You couldn't have had a very big plane land there. It probably was just as well they closed the airstrip, although I was a little irritated when it happened. Just like Jacksonville, it was very cheap to land there. People started building houses nearby and then started complaining

Now Butterknife, this used to be an airstrip.

because of the noise. But they built there knowing the airstrip was right in front of them, already there — you're not blind! You know about it. My brother John almost bought out there because he was looking for space because of his cows and horses.

John actually lived across the river in a little settlement called Fruit Cove, St. John's County. Boundary lines were strange back then. When you make boundary lines in an unmapped area, sometimes they get funny. For example, Coca-Cola, in establishing franchises, had some guy sitting somewhere in a swivel chair make Punta Gorda the distributor for our store. He had to come down the river and out the channel when we had a supplier right in Ft. Myers.

It was easy to navigate around the island in the old days. Quite simply, the roads were where you drove. The main road was along the beach (West Gulf) until it was washed away in the 1944 hurricane. Rabbit Road was two dirt tracks with tread grass in the middle. At dusk, there'd be 10,000 rabbits crossing that road! Another example is Sanibel-

Captiva Road. The people on Sanibel called it Captiva Road because that's where it went; the people on Captiva called it Sanibel Road for the same reason.

Shore Haven on a barge on its way to the Historical Village in October 2012.

On the bay, the road ran in front of the buildings (where the Sears kit house, Morning Glories, was, and its neighbor, Shore Haven, now relocated to the Historical Village), to the Post Office at Reed's Landing. On the Gulf it was the same way. When that road washed out and was moved back from the water to where it is now, the houses got sort of turned around — the back was the front and vice versa. I used to say the back doors became the front doors simply because the road moved.

Reed's Landing was about a mile west of Bailey Road. Today you would turn down Dixie Beach Boulevard, turn left at the end and go about one mile. Matthews Wharf was very close to where Bailey Road is now. That was demolished in the 1926 hurricane.

Ernest Kinzie was trying to build a dock where you could land heavy equipment at the end of Bailey Road. The main road used to run right down in front on the way to the Post Office. That was about all that was down there. By the time I came along there was a hotel there, which probably got knocked down in the 1944 hurricane, I'm not sure. There were two docks on the east end: Dixie Dock, which washed away and was rebuilt. It was the Kinzie Brothers steamer line in 1926. The steamboat would leave people at the dock and they would either go to the beach and shell and picnic or fish off the dock. There was also the lighthouse dock, docks at Wulfert, and various docks at the Woodrings'. There was a big long dock down Tarpon Bay Road with a big warehouse at the end of it. The dock itself was gone when I came along but the warehouse was still there until Hurricane Donna washed it away.

Capt. Leon at the helm of one of the steamboats that served the island.

Daddy built Sanibel Shores No. 1 subdivision in the 1920s with Donax running right through the middle of it. It was directly across from the homestead. The subdivision had been laid out on paper but never recorded as a subdivision. It was sold to Mr. Opre by Daddy. Opre outlined roads by Over Easy restaurant but never got to laying that out. The land included what is now the Bailey Tract. The Bailey Tract was never recorded as such but was going to be a subdivision, and so was the land behind the Over Easy restaurant. Sand filled it in. The gate on Island Inn Road is one of their ditches. There are houses down there now but there weren't until the 1950s or '60s. He dug ditches all over the place; some of them even had little wooden bridges across them. They were used by people for shortcuts for years, but nobody took care of the bridges.

Daddy built the Sanibel Shores subdivision directly across from the Homestead.

The joke used to be, "You want to buy a lot? Wait until the tide goes out." Literally, some land was sold that way. There were half-built structures all over the place – just the framework still sitting there. That's what happened to the island, boom and bust plus hurricanes and people just left in droves. I can think of at least 10 houses that were just sitting there, abandoned. Farming was the only thing to do and if the ground wasn't good and you lost your crop and lost your money, well, you usually left.

Captiva had its roads paved before the war, around 1940. Captiva and Sanibel had been harping on the county commission to fix our roads because they were wrecking our automobiles. They were washboard roads. Captiva's road was done first because they sort of whined, "Sanibel gets everything first." They paved from where the mail boat landed on Captiva almost to the bridge at Blind Pass. Remember, we were getting ready for war, and putting a road on a little old Godforsaken island wasn't a priority, so it was almost 10 years later before Sanibel got anything. But that didn't make any difference.

It was in the spring of 1947 when the first asphalt was put down on Sanibel. During the war, road equipment, barges, asphalt — everything — was commandeered by the federal government. The road ran from the ferry landing near the lighthouse up to just about where the schoolhouse was. The next year, 1948, they paved from there up to the Tarpon Bay/Periwinkle Way intersection.

I remember those two dates – the springs of 1947 and 1948 – because those were the two years I taught school in Virginia and the road was paved when I got back; it wasn't here when I left.

No roads had any real names over here; they acquired names. If Casa Ybel or Island Inn was on a road, then that's what it was called. As I said, the roads were where you drove. It was the insurance companies that had to have addresses. I think at first they used the name Sanibel Boulevard for Periwinkle Way. There were no addresses here. Mail carriers knew where everyone lived. A letter or package would be addressed to "J. Jones, The Matthews," or "F. Bailey, Sanibel, Florida." The name Sanibel Boulevard just didn't sound right to us. The words "trail," "road," "path" each convey a different picture and feeling. A trail is passable by foot. A road means some type of car can pass over it; of course, it was wagons and horses and mules back then. When you use the word "alley" that sounds like something behind your house where garbage is collected. "Lane" conveys a suburban place. But "Boulevard" is a wide open, fancy place. That is not Sanibel, and we didn't like it.

Then the county decided they needed to have a number system and a road name and they just made up names on their own. Priscilla Murphy, the first local Realtor, came to me and said, "That's not Sanibel Boulevard, we need to do something. It should be Periwinkle Way." Daddy planted periwinkles along the road between the coconut palms and pine trees — quite a lot of periwinkles. We got a bunch of people together who went before the county commissioners and, sure enough, they listened to us and named it Periwinkle Way. If you clear a place out now, sometimes the periwinkles will come up again, but there are not many. But that road was not named for the seashell, as many people think.

Priscilla was a prominent citizen and very involved in community affairs in those days, as you can see. She started out in a real estate firm with two women. The funny part about it was she dabbled in a whole bunch of things after her husband bought her a house. She threw pots. She started in the real estate business. None of us expected it to ever last, but it did. She became very successful.

When I used to compete in the Road Rally with Karen Bell, now the co-owner of Lily's Jewelry & Gallery, we had to find various and sundry things in the scavenger hunt. For example, teams would be given clues and then would have to drive around and count the number of manatee mailboxes or stop signs, things like that. One time we had to find "sightless eyes," and they turned out to be the headlights on an old wrecked car. Sometimes the rally organizers would also have questions for the teams at the end. One year my team would have won except that one of the questions was how Periwinkle Way got its name. I knew the answer, but the guy who helped make up the questions had written down the answer as "after the seashell," which was incorrect, and he just wouldn't give in. So we lost.

BUILDING A FIRE DEPARTMENT

We started a volunteer fire department because we needed one, it's that simple. I don't know how we got going but we did. We fought fires with shovels, and palmetto fronds we cut with knives; we used to try to stamp out the fires. From there the fire department just sort of evolved. Allen Nave was a volunteer chief for years and years and served that department for 50 years, retiring as commissioner.

Sanibel's volunteer firefighters with their first truck

First we got a fire truck and then we set up a system of alarms. Alarms were located at the store, East Rocks, the firehouse (where the antique shop is now on Periwinkle Way), and by Jimmy Jack's and Jean Jack's Casa Turquesa hotel toward the west part of the island. We had a series of radios: one at the store, one at East Rocks, and at the firehouse. If one was activated, they all went off. It was a form of communication for the fire department because the alarms were scattered all over the island.

I remember one time Joe Donahue and I were the first two to respond to an alarm. Joe was the Cockerills' son-in-law. It was about 5 p.m. and it kept going off from the alarm that was on West Gulf Drive. We finally figured it out: it was a Cuban radio station that came on the air about that time. It activated that station up there but didn't activate any other ones. We changed the frequency we were using so it wouldn't happen again.

Another time, we turned on the truck's siren and then couldn't turn it off. It's easy to panic when an alarm is continuously blaring and you can't turn it off. But Allen Nave got there, calm as can be the way he always was, and pulled the wires to turn it off.

It was a proud moment when we got our first real fire truck. It was followed by an unfortunate incident when the new truck was destroyed in a fire. Let me first state emphatically that I was not there! I'm not exactly sure what happened but suspect we either couldn't get it started or got it too close to where the fire was burning. But we got that truck replaced. I remember a story Daddy told about everyone struggling to get a piano out of a house before it burned – and once they finally succeeded and got it out, they left the piano too close to the house and it burned anyway.

Most fires were brush fires. We would drive out to a brush fire sometimes and let it burn because there was nothing we could do. When we did fight a fire we would have wet gunnysacks, like the material feed came in, to smother the fire – otherwise it was very flammable – and use two palm leaves put together to try to beat it down. My father told me they used to form bucket brigades, but most of that was just heroics.

Hurricane House burned in 1955

The Hurricane House fire in 1955 was one of the worst we experienced because that place was built out of what I call old Florida mahogany. It's really the old Florida yellow/long leaf pine. That wood is so hard you can't drive a nail in it. We had trouble fighting the fire just because of the heat; there really weren't any embers from that old pine. It did burn some of the underside of the eaves. At first we weren't even able to get water on it, the heat was so intense. But we completely saved one of the buildings. Paul Kearns had some trouble getting out, in fact. All we could do, really, was keep the fire from spreading. We saved the three-bedroom house next door. I was on the roof, Allen Nave was underneath me. The fascia was parched. We couldn't save the house, but we did do some good saving that second building.

In the 1950s on Mother's Day, Casa Ybel Road got involved in a brush fire. I was coming back from church and heading to the Island Inn or something. I saw a little fire burning and I had my good clothes on so I tried to get it but couldn't. It was dead grass. Sometimes you beat it and a spark flies and you make it worse. It was very dry and there was nothing I could do about it. That fire got out of control. We fought it all afternoon.

A volunteer fire department is a very informal thing and we just raised money by begging and borrowing. To buy the truck, a Fire District was required where you had commissioners; I think we got some help from the state. Those commissioners have taxing authority just like the county commissioners – and they still do today. They could go up to 10 mills (a tenth of a point).

When we formed the fire district, we needed that taxing authority and a budget. We had to have three commissioners and they had to be appointed by the governor, but the governor didn't know anybody. Nine times out of 10, a governor doesn't know anybody. So the people on the island appointed me to go and essentially tell the governor's liaison who to appoint. I talked to the attorney who was the representative of the governor here in Lee County. Back in those days it was all Democrat; now of course it's all Republican.

We submitted three names for the commissioners: Martin Hiers, Pat Murphy and Tom Billheimer. Tommy Shands, the governor's representative, recommended them, and the reason he did that was because I recommended them to him. Allen Nave and Dave Wooster were also instrumental in forming the fire district.

I guess I did have a lot to do with the early fire department on Sanibel.

THE BAILEY HOMESTEAD

Going to the homestead now, the land doesn't look much like it did when I was growing up. My father told me he could stand on the steps at the homestead and see Gray Gables (originally just called The Gables), the Nutt sisters' home, which today still sits on the same piece of property on West Gulf Drive but closer to the road instead of on the beach. When I was growing up, if we looked out the attic window, we could see the gulf. Never in my time could

Part of the homestead grounds

you look across the whole island from any location, but it was a lot sparser than it is today.

At the homestead, there was a citrus grove, thatches of palmetto, gardens, the barn with mules, and the windmill. There was also what we called "the lot," which was a small enclosure with no grass where we'd put the gate up so animals couldn't wander away in the morning before we had a chance to hook them up. I remember when we would drive mules through the grove and they would see white sand, they would shy away and you couldn't get them to go through because of the gopher holes – they could break a leg.

We never called our home the Donax house, by the way, although some people tend to call it that now. There wasn't even a Donax Street when it was built or when I was growing up. That road became Donax Street when the subdivision was built; Mother named all those roads over there. In my time, it was just "the street to the beach," just like Bailey Road was "the road to the store." Nor was the homestead ever called the Tea Pot, as some have written. There were times Uncle Ernest called it the Smudge Pot, though, because of all the mosquito pots we burned in the house.

The homestead is a typical island house. You build the house, then you build a porch. You need more room, so you enclose that porch. Then you build another porch – and then enclose that – and build another porch. My father had the house built in 1896 shortly

Above: The kitchen wing

Right: Palm room to the left

after he arrived on Sanibel. It cost $500; a porch would have cost another $15, so he didn't get a porch. It was just a plain square four-room house with no attic.

In 1908 Daddy added the wing with the bathroom and the house got running water. There was a water tower with a base of cypress wood. I have no idea when the dormer was added. the house has had three different roof lines over time.

I never have been able to figure out when they added the kitchen, but it was likely prior to 1908. When I was growing up, a screen was across the walkway to the kitchen area, and the kitchen was really closed in. I believe about that time the back stairs were added by the kitchen. There was a breezeway between the house and kitchen; and another between the house and the new wing for my parents, and that one was screened.

In 1919 when Daddy got married, he took one wall out to make one big room to serve as a larger living room, added a breezeway, bedroom and closet, and built another bathroom. The entrance

Palm room where Daddy kept plants.

Porch interior

77

and porch were demolished to enable us to add a new bedroom. A whole back nursery was built five years later. We rebuilt the porch in 1960. Hurricane Donna had damaged the old porch enough so that it had to be torn down. We were going to use the insurance money to put up a garage but my wife Pauline wanted a porch instead. Much later in 1968, more rooms were added and the attic was added too. In my time, what had been Uncle Ernest's room became my den, which was filled with books on shelves my second wife Adelaide had built.

The windmill, which was made of steel, pumped water to an overhead tank for gravity to feed water to the house. There were banana trees underneath it and when it overflowed, it helped to keep them wet. There was a walkway all around the tank where water was pumped in from the windmill – pipes also went down

Mary Mead cleaning the attic

from the bottom of it that led wherever you wanted the water to go. If you used too much water or didn't get much wind, then you had to go without water. We also had two cypress cisterns, or tanks, about two feet above ground – one was next to the overhead tank right beside the kitchen, another one was in the corner between Mother and Daddy's room and the nursery, at least three feet off the ground, with a pipe just stuck through the wall. The tanks were very close to the house; the windmill was about 150 yards from the house. Windmill water was for bathing, washing dishes, and watering the plants. But if you didn't have much rain you had to watch them too. Our cisterns were cylindrical wooden cypress. Some people had cement. Either way, water could be a problem if the wind didn't blow, and if it didn't rain of course the cisterns didn't fill up.

The windmill water was a different system from the cistern water. The cistern water came into the bathroom and we had a bucket under the sink to catch the leaks. That water was as hard as a rock. If you put it in a glass and let it evaporate, the glass was covered with white. Mother would use it for washing our hair and some clothing.

The windmill was destroyed in the 1944 hurricane. Daddy bought some blades to fix it but never activated the thing again. We had what we called a standpipe that we only used sometimes for tender first plantings. It was the easiest way to get water to the field.

Also on the property were a turkey pen, a chicken house — its remains are still there — a mule barn and a packing house. The packing house blew down in 1935. We packed vegetables but not during my time, at least not within my memory.

We never had any pigs; very few people did. Charlie Carter had some much later on, after the war, on the corner of Periwinkle Way and Tarpon Bay Road near where Bailey's store is today. Almost everyone had a chicken house, for eggs as well as for eating. My mother roasted or baked a chicken or turkey on Sundays. A lot of people fried chicken but we didn't eat a tremendous amount of fried food – but sometimes fried chicken and fried fish were allowed.

It was quiet then. All you heard was the rattle-rattle-rattle of some cars passing on the washboard road that became Periwinkle. The buzz of mosquitoes, too, of course. You get toughened up to the bugs. If a carpenter hits his thumb, he says a few choice words and then goes on and finishes his business. That's what bugs were like for me. We had big brown spiders in the bedroom. They would both eat the mosquitoes and catch them in their webs. They would eventually form a big white sac and a billion babies would come out. We liked the spiders. The only kind of spiders we really hated were gold spiders. They weave a very sticky web and we used to walk through the swamps all the time and we'd walk across an opening and get the whole sticky web in our faces. There's also a crab spider, big as a fingernail with a very hard shell. We liked those. But I never heard of anyone keeping spiders on purpose to reduce the numbers of mosquitoes.

We hated gold spiders because of their sticky webs.

The mosquitoes don't like wind and dark, cool, quiet places. In those days you would see no bushes around the doors, which would lessen the number of bugs. But you get in a lime grove – the trees are big, there's no breeze, and you know the mosquitoes are going to bite you so you put on an undershirt and a shirt – long sleeves of course – and then the sandspurs were thick in there, and the thorns! All citrus has some thorns but lime trees have massive thorns. You would have to put on canvas leggings. You perspire so much your shirt sticks to your back, so it doesn't work anyway – the mosquitoes go right through it. So there you are in a lime grove, your fingers are full of pricks, you're hot as Hades, and about that time you must have stepped in an ants' nest and they go underneath your leggings and your legs are on fire. You can't do anything about it. You can't get to them. And then you think, "Well, nothing else can happen." You squat down to get a lime on a low branch and a big sandspur gets behind your knee. That's my definition of hell.

In spite of some of these stories that make it sound like life was so difficult, I kept hoping I could move back to the homestead, but that just wasn't going to happen. My first wife Pauline was happy living at the homestead, I believe. Adelaide's family had a house

on the gulf and would spend time there but within a few years, she wanted to move on to a more modern house, and the same thing happened with my current wife June, which I guess I can understand. Pauline lived there six years and Adelaide lived there eight, the entire tenure of our marriage. I lived there by myself for eight years before I married June, and that was a special time for me. I didn't especially like living alone but people came and went – the children and their friends, and John's daughter Angela stayed for some months. I didn't give the house very good care, though. In an old house, you can sneeze on one side of the house and feel it on the other.

I feel a big part of me is wrapped up in that house, with Mother and Daddy and my childhood on Sanibel. If I had to pick a favorite time there, it would be before 1935 when I didn't have any worries except being forced to eat spinach.

Even the vegetation at the homestead has memories for me, even a tree, any silly little thing. I feel at peace there, and it was hard to leave. I finally left around 1988, when June and I moved into a house in The Dunes. My current wife June didn't like living at the homestead. Women seem to have an aversion to whatever another female has done, including my mother. They just want to change everything and I didn't want to change anything. So it just didn't work.

The house was built in the old style, too, to maximize air circulation. June would find it hot one morning and cold the next, and she just didn't like it. I suppose we could have done some renovations, added central air conditioning, insulation – but it's an old house and it was not built for air conditioning. So we moved out after about six years to the house in The Dunes where our children Tom and Linda Stevens live now.

I was upset to leave, there's no two ways about it. I wish I were back there, but I could never convince my wife. Even though you can't live in the past, it's nice to reminisce sometimes. I wish the land could have stayed the way it was. The property is wonderful, with a big, huge yard where the citrus groves were. The Sanibel-Captiva Conservation Foundation, which now owns the land and the house, is a very good caretaker of land. They have never had to care for a building before but they seemed to want it. It's been through a lot, that house; it's gone through hurricanes. It's a pretty tough old buzzard.

The homestead circa 1896   **The homestead, 2012, with a SCCF facelift**

Cleaning out the house was an overwhelming task for my children and their families, their cousin Angela, and me. I get frustrated that I no longer have the physical strength to just get it cleaned out – it bothered me to see it the way it had become after years of neglect.

Among the hundreds of books, trunks, and other things, I saw a pile of baby shoes with the names of their owners – my children – written on the bottoms. Noticing there were no shoes for Mary Mead, she said she didn't have any because she always went barefoot. That's not 100 percent true; we would never have let her go to church or school without shoes.

I haven't read them all, but I've read a lot.

There must have been hundreds of books in there – two rooms with floor-to-ceiling shelves, all full. Books are very precious to me, so those had to be packed up and I intend to go through them all. I'll confess I haven't read them all by a long shot, but I've read a lot of them. We never had a Victrola, but there were a lot of records in the house, too – 33s, 45s, and 78s. We used to borrow radios. Uncle Ernest wanted to hear the operas and stuff and winter people would leave radios in our car. I still love the big band music, particularly Glenn Miller. I remember listening to the big fight in the guest room of the house on a borrowed radio: the second Joe Louis/Max Schmeling fight in 1938. I went to get a chair and was dragging it up – and the fight was over. I never even got to sit down. It lasted all of two minutes and four seconds before Louis won by a knockout.

We also found shipping crates, heavy wooden ones, with those colorful old-fashioned labels that will be put to use in the produce section of the general store. It was a surprise when we opened the largest of the crates and discovered one of the beautiful labels for my grandfather's tobacco brands. There were a couple of cardboard packing crates there, and I remember Daddy told me when he first received a shipment of groceries packed in cardboard, he sent it back – he thought it was inferior to the wooden crates. I used to build those same wooden crates for the tomatoes. There are still wooden crates today, particularly for produce, but they're made of very thin material you can almost bend and break.

I also came across Pauline's wedding dress, stockings and purse — and the cake topper — while I was wandering around the house. I remembered proposing to Pauline while we were sitting on a dock in front of her house at Twin Palm – it might have been Palms back then. John Engle, her father, planted two coconut nuts so close

that when they came up, there were two palms together. It's a wonder he didn't bury me if he was burying nuts! One of his best fertilizers were 'coons. He'd shoot them and bury them by the palm tree.

Many of these old things were in the attic all these years – the attic Daddy and his brothers sometimes slept in, which is hard to imagine now. It must have been hotter than hell. But when you're in the heat all day long, it becomes bearable, as opposed to now when we're in air conditioning all day long. The attic is huge, equal to the footprint of the original house. There were floorboards that were even kind of loose; it was just dead storage. So we hadn't seen the older things that were up there since they were put away. I know I hadn't seen Pauline's things since some wonderful ladies who helped me after she died considerately stored her things away. That's a long time.

I'm not surprised we didn't find an old radio up in that attic. Daddy didn't have much to do with radios. Later on, after lunch he used to take a brief nap and then listened to Helen Trent.

These are stories that came back to me as we cleaned out the homestead. We came across my Mother's trunk and opened it to find some delicate lingerie and beautiful white gloves. That trunk was in our bathroom behind a curtain and served to hold her clothes. There were also Uncle Ernest's and Sam's trunks, and the two smaller trunks I used for going away to school. I got them second-hand; who could afford to buy new stuff? I don't know that those trunks look any worse now than they did then and that was 75 years ago.

We found a total of 12 trunks when we finally finished cleaning out the homestead. The only trunks I can identify are the two that I had, Mother's trunk, and Sam's. One trunk has Uncle Ernest's name on it, too, so I guess that's five out of 12. Uncle Ernest did a lot of

We found 12 trunks in the homestead — all full of stories long forgotten.

Mary Mead tries to open Uncle Ernest's trunk.

traveling, and people dressed for travel in those days. I don't know if he owned a necktie but he must have. I think I have seen pictures of him in a necktie. You would think there would be some modern stuff up there – it probably got pitched out.

I also found my old Army boots. I used them after I came back and wore them until I wore them out. So much has been saved that I would have just tossed. My former desk still contains bank statements, laundry receipts – so much paper! There's even a fraternity paddle, but it's Ned Crawford's, my second cousin who was killed in the war. I never got a paddle; they cost money and I couldn't afford it.

If Mary Mead remembers going barefoot, it could be because we didn't have air conditioning until she was six years old, around 1967. My second wife Adelaide liked old things and

This was my home office for many years.

antiques and made her own mark on the house. If we were anywhere near an antique shop, the car automatically turned in. We used to go bottle hunting, too, and Mary Mead has a lot of the bottles. I think both Pauline and Adelaide were happy in the house, as far as I know.

I hope the children were happy. We had dogs and a ton of indoor/outdoor cats that would come and go as they jolly well pleased. We used hardware cloth to protect the screen against dogs' paws and little kids but the cats could open it. Of course, you're not supposed to push on the door, that's what the screens are there for. There was very little traffic and lots of room for the animals to run around.

Dogs have been a wonderful part of my life, in fact, my favorite toy as a little boy was a stuffed Airedale dog I took to bed every night. I have two shih tzus now, MaiLi and SinTu – dust mops! We don't have to have brooms, we just stick handles in their backs.

The dogs I had growing up were "Heinz 57" dogs, like every little boy. We also got a dog from a woman who lived in Louisville or someplace, an Irish terrier named Goofus (we called him Goof). His big thing was chasing cars. He was chasing this Model T one time and

I found my old army boots which I used for years — and Sam's football cleats.

it ran over him. Apparently the car ran over the dog's abdomen area and his chest was grossly swollen when I got to him. After a while the swelling went down and he got up and went about his business – slowly. Those Model Ts didn't weigh a lot and it was going very slowly. John had a lot of hunting dogs. There were always at least two cats as pets, too. We didn't have a cat in the barn, believe it or not, because we had chickens, for eggs and eating. When I first got married, Pauline and I had a boxer and one of her puppies. There's nothing like a dog.

One of our cats sleeps on the bed, maybe guarding the shoes hanging over the door.

We had cats all the time. You could get a cat anywhere. Feral cats would have kittens someplace and we would go out and find one and in a very short time, the kitten was completely tame. Nobody knew what spay and neuter was in those days. We had a mother cat that had kittens three or four times a year and one time she had them in my bed. They would come and go. There were no litter boxes; if we had one, it was sand from out in the yard. The bottom of the screen door was worn and they could get their paws in there and open the door so they came and went as they wanted.

There's a semi-organized group of people on the island now who want a dog park and keep trying to get one. I can see why the city says no. Land has gotten so ridiculously high-priced on Sanibel, and land is hard to find. But I don't know where the dogs are supposed to run. Barry Gordon, who owns the print shop The Big Red Q, is a Kiwanian who hosts the dog people at his house in the winter, about six people with their dogs. The street, Conch, is only about 300 yards to a dead end with just 11 houses on it. It's the only time the dogs get to run free. That makes me feel bad; dogs need to run and that's the only time they get a chance.

When my children were growing up in the homestead, whenever there were heavy rains, they would take the tractor and pull each other behind it over the water. I've been told recently they called it "redneck waterskiing." I didn't know about it until much later on. We had one TV that you practically needed binoculars to see.

I assume the Honey House, which I sometimes called the Swiss Chalet, was built long before 1919 but I don't really know. Half of it was referred to as "The Shop," where Daddy had tools and used to build things. It was bare studs with no ceiling. The other half was servants' quarters. I suppose you call them nannies these days. They helped take care of us. After there were no more nannies, we started the bee business, made frames and repaired equipment and stored extra honey.

When it was a working honey house, we used to take the combs out of the hives and with a hot knife, slice the caps off them. Then centrifugal force would extract the honey and we would strain it, all by hand. The other half of the little house was finished inside with a bathroom and a little bedroom. Adelaide was trying to get a young lady to come over from Switzerland to help with the kids but it never materialized. Later on, people did stay there. A friend of my daughter Anne came to spend the night and she was still there six months later. She worked at Duncan's which is now the Blue Giraffe restaurant. She used to cook for us, so we were grateful to have her there.

The hurricane destroyed the citrus grove in 1944. Daddy planted a garden after that and some more trees, but I never cared for them properly. There was a fence around the property in those days – it was a farm and the fence delineated what was farm and what was yard. We had big coconut trees and palmettos. We cut the grass with a laddy boy, swinging it back and forth. If you did that for a day, you had a day's work in!

CHAPTER 3
I LEAVE HOME

LEAVING SANIBEL: PREP SCHOOL AND COLLEGE

In all, I was away from Sanibel about 13 years during the winters, eight of those for school, then the Army, then a short stint teaching and working in a lumber mill. I left just after my mother died in 1935. I always came back in the summers for at least weeks at a time, except for one summer when I wasn't able to afford to come home. I returned to Sanibel full-time and for good in 1948.

My heart was always here even when I wasn't. It was the same for my brothers to a degree. As youngsters we wanted to get away: it was hot, there were mosquitoes, sandspurs, there weren't any girls, no air conditioning — and you want the life of luxury. Well, I haven't found it yet.

Daddy still felt like a Virginian, as I mentioned earlier and at first he wanted me to go to Staunton Military Academy in Virginia. To go to Fort Myers High School you really had to move to Fort Myers because the ferry schedule didn't accommodate the school schedule. Daddy couldn't move the family there because his business was on Sanibel, and Mother didn't want me running around the streets of Fort Myers.

In spite of the fact that Daddy did very well during the 1920s, he took an awful beating once the hurricane hit and the land boom busted. He still had relatives in Staunton, so I think that was a factor in him wanting me to go there. Then something happened with the school, or he learned something about the school — I never found out what it was — and Daddy did a 180-degree turn-around and didn't want me to go there anymore.

> **They thought we were sissies and we had to straighten them out on that.**

All of us have a tendency to do this: you think of something and then you get attached to the idea. Daddy didn't really know anything about the school in Staunton. Then apparently he found out something and it changed his mind. It was when my mother died and we went up there to bury her that we went to look at Augusta Military Academy. I have never known why but suddenly he decided on Augusta. The biggest thing wrong with it was the cost — it was very expensive; even the uniform was too expensive. It was just out of the question for me to go there.

Daddy then turned his attention to Virginia Episcopal School in Lynchburg. Bishop Robert Carter Jett founded this school for people who couldn't afford fancy prep schools, and that's where I ended up going after Daddy changed his mind about military school.

I was a pretty green kid at 14. We island boys were pretty well isolated from so-called social mores and niceties of the day and in most ways were not very sophisticated. I was a little hick boy. Most of us down here were scrubby guys. I don't know if any of the boys had any shoes on in school. My two brothers and I had short pants on — none of the other boys ever did. They thought we were sissies and we had to straighten them out on that.

In the fall I went up on the train to Virginia Episcopal School with grandmother. She probably took me all the way to Lynchburg. At that point in my life I don't think I'd ever spent a night that I wasn't with my mother, father, grandmother, or Aunt Char.

We left on a Sunday. We were in a Pullman and Granny wanted to play cards, and I remonstrated because my mother wouldn't let us play cards or even read the funny papers on Sunday. Granny said she'd straighten it out with Mother. In the summertime we used to play double solitaire with Granny. We had an ongoing backgammon game with Mother and my two brothers. And she always had a jigsaw puzzle going. It's amazing to me that to this day we sell an awful lot of jigsaw puzzles in the store.

Although I missed my family, I just fell in love with prep school. I was never homesick. I was always glad to get back home, though, and every time I did, I didn't think I was ever going to go back to school. It cost $600, which covered room, board, and tuition. You had to pay $20 for school supplies and books. But somehow my father was able to scrape up the money for the tuition with some help from Uncle Clark on my mother's side. I made

Hallway at prep school

$75 a year waiting tables and another $75 picking up laundry, so I worked both jobs for $150 a year. Then I was offered a job in the school store for the same amount – $150 a year. But they worked you to death: mornings, recesses, lunches, after school, an hour before supper – even the 10-minute study hall break.

I liked everything about school, even though it was sort of Spartan. My bedroom was more like a horse stall, with a three-quarter wall between me and the next guy, nothing on the front, an iron chair and bed. The wardrobe was small — one side was shelves, one side for hanging, and it locked. We had to keep things clean, too. We were well disciplined. When the bell rang in the morning we had better get up; our feet had to be on the floor.

I was too young to worry about the difference in the weather moving from Sanibel to Virginia. I was 14 and had never seen snow. The freshmen were always required to get up at 6 a.m. and close all the windows in the dorm and the steam heat would come up. That was our job. It was real cold one morning at one guy's place and the head counselor asked, "Is the snow sticking?" I had no idea what he was talking about. Snow sticking? What a foreign concept to a boy from Sanibel. I stuck my head out the window and said, "Yes, it is!" I realized later it wasn't, it was just a few little snow flurries that were falling.

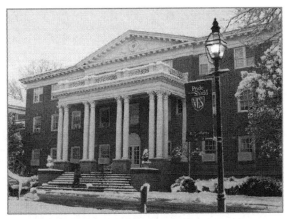

Virginia Episcopal School

When I was going to prep school – and even during college and my teaching days – I spent time at a cousin's house in Richmond. Cousin Lillian Crawford was on Mother's side of the family. School vacations are different now than they were then; you couldn't stay at the school. Spring vacation was to start and it was too expensive to come home, so I spent it with her.

During summers I was able to go home, Daddy's secretary Miss Lula – who was still working for Daddy when I was in college –tried to teach me to type. I did fairly well but ruined it all when I went back to school writing sports stories for the newspaper. I got to doing two-finger typing.

My prep school was very small; everyone lived in just two buildings. We knew everybody on the campus slightly, or at least knew their names. Walking around the campus, from the janitor to the president to classmates, you always spoke to everyone. The greeting used to be, "What do you say?" just like now people say, "How ya' doin'." I told my prep school friends that Sanibel was an island with a ferry boat that stopped running at 5 p.m., no movie theater, no filling station, no furniture store, no barber, no beauty shop, and no drugstore. My buddies couldn't comprehend it. I remember a time one boy couldn't sleep because he had a mosquito bite – one bite! I told him how we'd wake up in the morning with blood spots on the sheets from all the mosquito bites we'd gotten through the night. When I heard him complaining about one bite, I just burst out laughing. I was country.

Education and sports were very important in our family, but Daddy knew nothing about football, so being a dutiful son, I didn't go out for football. In such a small school, though, the feeling about the boys who didn't play football was that they were sissies. So I went out for boxing to put that notion to rest, and I won some matches. That changed their minds. I boxed at 155 pounds; I think that's about a welterweight today. I competed in track meets, too, and thought I was reasonably fast but didn't realize how fast until I got in a couple of things and won.

We had two hours of compulsory study hall every night (study hall was called the Imposition Period). If you got behind in some of your grades, you were required to go there and study. Then supper was at 6:30 p.m.

There was a counselor system, three to every dorm floor. They served as assistants to the master, and it was a counselor who sat during the Imposition Period. Those people were allowed to stay up until 11 p.m., they had tables with lamps and were allowed to study there instead of study hall. I was a counselor for two years.

I was a bad boy, though. We had a demerit system and if you got 15 demerits within a month's time, you had to work them off and you couldn't leave the school grounds. Not leaving the school grounds meant you couldn't go to town; guys who were dating couldn't see their girls. You were allowed three demerits a week — the school week was Tuesday through Saturday — before you were penalized.

> ## I thought I was tough, but I had blisters inside my blisters.

You had to walk off your demerits, and it wasn't easy. You could work instead, and I'd rather work than walk — or so I thought. The school was building a new baseball field and the ground was full of rocks. Our work was to break up those rocks. That doesn't sound like much but when you break them up using a sledge hammer, it gets heavy. I thought I was tough, but I had blisters inside my blisters.

Sam was three years behind me, so when it was time for him to go to high school, Mother was gone and therefore so were her concerns about her boys roaming the streets of Fort Myers. People were still concerned but didn't have much choice. I was using the family's money going to Lynchburg. So Sam did go to live in Fort Myers and attend school there. Daddy chose people for Sam to stay with. Sam told one story of a woman landlord who spent forever adding up his breakfast tab — he almost missed the mail boat because of it. Breakfast was 25 cents, and there she was with this little stub of a pencil writing 25 cents at a time, then five plus five equals 10, plus five equals 15, plus five equals 20, carry the two. "I ought to know this," she said, while Sam's rushing to make the boat. Keeping tabs on Sam was like trying to harness a raging rhino, so I guess Mother was right to have concerns about letting us run around in Fort Myers.

By the time Sam was in school, though, things had mellowed a bit regarding Daddy's feelings about football. I was already playing some, and Sam started playing a little bit and broke the ice.

Daddy did his best to support Sam and go to his high school games. Daddy's eyesight was not very good, and you can't tell who a player is in a helmet anyway, except for their number. After a while when the players all left the field, Daddy thought the game was over; of course, it was half-time. He asked, "Well, how long IS the game?" We told him there were 45 minutes to go. Daddy called a huddle a "muddle." Sam thought he played a pretty good game, and when it was over Daddy said to him, "Did you play?" I doubt whether he knew which team was which.

I played football, although badly.

My school only had about 120 students in it and about 121 of them played football. It wasn't compulsory that you played but nearly everyone did. There were just a few who didn't and I didn't really like it much anyway. But the next year I went out for football. Damn if I didn't wrench my knee and have my entire leg in a cast for weeks. I was out for I don't know how long. I didn't think I was ever going to play again. Even though I wasn't a very good player and didn't get in many games, my classmates kept saying, "Come play." That's just the way it was. Later on in the Army it was the same thing. Still later, it was sandlot playing in Richmond when I was working in the lumber yard. I believe I played more there than I did in school.

So prep school gave me a good background. When I went there my first year, I weighed 145 pounds. When I came back the next year, I'd grown two inches and weighed 140 pounds.

When I went to college I didn't know what the heck I wanted to be. Farming appealed to me, the big wide open spaces of the amber waves of grain.

I got an academic scholarship to Hampden-Sydney for $50. Back in 1939 that was a lot of money. Seventy years ago $50 made a difference. Hampden-Sydney is the 10th oldest college in the U.S., founded in 1776. The campus is 660 acres about 60 miles southwest of Richmond, Virginia. The National Youth Administration helped out, getting students like me certain jobs sorting dirty socks in the gym and that sort of thing. I worked as a waiter, and it was a little different than dining at the Ritz, I can tell you that.

The first year I didn't matriculate until late and the dorms were full, so I stayed in a rooming house. No food was provided and it was eight or 10 people just on the second floor. Some were seniors, four were freshman. One guy, a senior, had a car and was in a single room by himself. I had little or nothing to do with my roommate after my freshman year – maybe he wasn't even in school after that. We just didn't have very much in common. Two sisters ran the house, one was named Emma Venerable, and I can't remember her sister's name. They were two old ladies, one deaf as a post and her ears used to ring all the time. They were from the old Southern style and invited everyone to Thanksgiving dinner. They had a black man who was maid, cook, and all that sort of stuff. The feast they put on for Thanksgiving was unbelievable. I think that's the only time I ever ate there, though; I always ate at the school.

There were no restaurants anywhere around. The closest one was in Farmville, Virginia. There were some filling stations and juke joints – we would get candy bars when we were supposed to be studying.

The reason I was late in matriculating was because I didn't think I was going to be able to go to school at all. Uncle Harry and Daddy got together and I thought at least I could go for one year. Tuition included classes and room and board.

When I finally did live in the college dorms during my sophomore and junior years, the thing I remember is they had fuses that would burn out and we would stick a penny in there. How we didn't burn the place down, I don't know. I lived in a rooming house for freshman year, and my senior year I lived in a fraternity house.

I took conventional courses: chemistry, algebra – I don't know why they would put me in there because I had the entire advanced math course in prep school: algebra, geometry, and trigonometry. I ended up taking one or two years of psychology, Spanish, literature, and physics. I remember I didn't have to study too hard. I didn't even buy a book for algebra. I don't know how I got away with it. But chemistry was new and I almost flunked it. You could drop a course, so that's what I did. I eventually took it later and passed it by the skin of my teeth.

We were required to study the Bible for two years or we wouldn't graduate. It was a Presbyterian college and we used the American Standard Bible, not the King James Version. Now, when I die, if anybody wants to read the 23rd Psalm at my service from anything but the King James Bible, lightning is going to strike him:

The Lord is my shepherd; I shall not want.
He maketh me to lie down in green pastures: he leadeth me beside the still waters.
He restoreth my soul: he leadeth me in the paths of righteousness for his name's sake.
Yea, though I walk through the valley of the shadow of death,
I will fear no evil: for thou art with me; thy rod and thy staff they comfort me.
Thou preparest a table before me in the presence of mine enemies;
thou anointest my head with oil; my cup runneth over.
Surely goodness and mercy shall follow me all the days of my life,
and I will dwell in the house of the Lord forever.

My Bible teacher was called Snapper, although not to his face, but he must have known. That was because he kept sticking his tongue out like a snapper turtle. We were not allowed to cross our legs in class because it could scratch the chair in front. The building was relatively new, so this was a concern. But in the front row you could cross your legs and being a Bailey – "B" – I was in the front row.

I never heard of a major, just a BA or BS, and they weren't that different. I took the BS and I think what I ended up with is what "BS" stands for outside of school. I just got through by the skin of my teeth, probably because I didn't apply myself as much as I should have. If I could graduate college, anybody could.

College man

We had a strict honor code, though. On everything you submitted, you had to write, "I have neither given nor received any help on this work." In prep school we had the Honor Committee. I don't think they had the ultimate authority, but we had guys who cheated or stole, and they got kicked out of school. When I taught there, I had guys I had to take home who had been expelled. Those weren't pleasant journeys.

Sometimes we'd gather in somebody's room for a bull session, we called it. I don't know what we'd talk about, all kinds of things.

I got my nickname in one of those sessions. A classmate and fraternity brother would say to me, "Moon Mullins (a comic strip character), you banjo-eyed bum," and from then on, I was Moon. Why he picked me out of 10 guys in the room to say that to, I have no idea. Nobody called anybody by their first names anyway. In the football program I was listed as M. Bailey. I never heard the name Francis after that. People from the college years who visited or wrote me afterwards always called me Moon.

I was pretty shy in college and just had one or two dates the entire time – and those were arranged by someone else. I don't remember too much about her, but there was a girl called Pogie; she was the Bible teacher's daughter. We didn't wear face masks when we played football in those days, and somebody hit me upside the face with an elbow and I had a mouse on my left eye. For some reason she was out there and I was talking to her. Pogie was sympathetic with me because of my mouse – which I got in the last play of the last game.

My fraternity was Kappa Sigma. Kappa Sigma is focused on the four cornerstones of fellowship, leadership, scholarship and service. It is a values-based men's fraternity. The fraternity was a place you could get away from the roaring crowd. It was good fellowship, and most people joined one. There were students who didn't join. You had to be asked to join a fraternity. It was called "rushing," just as it is today. The members would lay out the red carpet, so to speak. Our fraternity house had burned down the year before so we didn't even have a fraternity house. We got another one built pretty quickly.

Our chapter was somewhat self-governing. Kappa Sigma has a big headquarters in Charlottesville, Virginia. I don't know what it's really all about but they do things, have a publication they send out, and they have a Man of the Year. One year it was Hoagie Carmichael, another it was Edward R. Murrow. All the members call each other brothers. Harry Bertosa on Sanibel, and Jamie Parkerson who started the Bubble Room on Captiva, were Kappa Sigma brothers.

The relationships – the bond of a fraternity – last a lifetime.

They did have big parties but I wasn't drinking anything in those days, absolutely nothing. But guess who always had to tap the beer keg at every party? I did!

We had a series of Friday night dances. I don't think they started until 9 p.m. and went to about 1 a.m. When you took a girl to the dance, anyone could cut in, never mind signing a dance card like they did in the old days. A girl that didn't get cut in on was a very unpopular girl. In college I only had a date to a dance one time in eight years because I was very shy. And there was a tea dance after every football game on Saturday. Dances were never on the campus in my early college years.

There was a comedy club that looked like an old deserted barn but we actually had Jimmy Dorsey there – which cost money, of course, so I didn't get to see him. Eventually that old barn burned down and we had a big conference to decide what to do. Our fraternity used the gymnasium after that, but not all of them did.

One year I got to play in only one game.

People say the movie Animal House was slightly exaggerated – slightly my foot! There was no animosity between members of the fraternities; maybe a little bit with the non-Greeks but not a whole lot. We got along fine. Some of my best friends were in other fraternities. We went to other houses, to their parties, and vice versa. When we went on football trips we would go to other colleges out of town and you could notice the animosity. We were sort of "half-way" welcomed.

In college, once again everybody urged me to go out for the football team. Come spring practice the guys talked me into it again. It was a little school, just 400 students, so I went out. I didn't even have a locker; I threw my things in the corner of the gym. I thought that was the end of the line. One year I only got in one play in one game, that was all. But I practiced and scrimmaged all year. I never started but two games in college. I played guard and was about 200 pounds underweight for that position. I weighed 172 and might have been a running back. Although we had recruited scholarship players, today I don't think you would find the walk-on players we had then. Anyone who wanted to could go out and play football. It wasn't the coach, it was my fellow classmates who urged me to play. I was putting out 102 percent. Again I thought that was the end of it — but they talked me into going out for the team again. The next three years, I didn't have to be talked into it.

As early as the end of my freshman year, the fact that I wasn't worth a damn was obvious. Nevertheless, every time spring practice came, just as they did in prep school, my classmates urged me to go out again, and I didn't do too badly. But when I got out of college, where was I going to play? In the Army of course. I stayed with them for a while but they soon started getting some good players, so I no longer belonged on that team.

Later on, in the Army, they had a team in Salt Lake City and were recruiting a football team so I went out and played again. They soon told me, "Go out and play tiddlywinks." Then after I wasn't playing anymore, the team asked again if I would play. They had a very different reason this time: they were going to be playing in a prison; I jumped at the chance to play anyway.

That prison really made an impression on me. Its doors were like bank vault doors; you went through one, heard it clang shut loudly, and then you went through another and heard that second loud clang shutting you in there. When those heavy doors closed shut I can't describe the feeling that came over me. It was an eerie feeling, I'll tell you. We played in a field, if you can call it that — the top of the table in my office is softer than that field. There wasn't a blade of grass on it.

After all that and teaching school for two years, I was in Richmond in the fall of 1948 working in a lumber yard that had a sandlot football team and I went out for that. I played quite a bit — finally — and some of the guys I played with in college were on those teams.

I did make my letter the last year in college but that was the only time. That was an important thing because you had to play so much. I probably made my letter because a good many guys were off to war. And Sam and I had the chance to play football together at Hampden-Sydney; I was a senior and Sam was a freshman. The following year he went to Georgia.

I loved playing, but I would never encourage young people to play football today. It's ceased to be a game. There's no such thing as a college team, they're just farms. It's like the minor leagues in baseball. Half of them don't speak English — and I don't mean a foreign language, I mean poor English. I don't feel the same way about baseball.

Connie Mack

One memory about baseball that sticks in my mind is when Connie Mack – the first Connie Mack, the man who spent 40 years managing the Philadelphia Athletics and grandfather to the politician we know today – came to Fort Myers. This was quite a bit before 1963 because I remember the ferry was still running. When I was still a boy in the late '20s and early '30s, he was manager and owner of the Philadelphia Athletics and wintered in Fort Myers. The Athletics were a powerful team then, world champions for two or three years. They won nine American League Championships, and led Mr. Mack straight to Cooperstown and induction into the baseball Hall of Fame. Now, 30 years later, Charlie Knapp owned Casa Ybel where they would have fish fries. We used our car to transport some of the players there because there was only so much transportation. Connie Mack came over on the boat and Jimmie Foxx (the first baseman known as "The Beast") sat in the front with Uncle Ernest. But I met Mr. Mack in the Casa Marina restaurant, which was owned by Betty Sears, Mike Billheimer's aunt, who ran the Island Inn's dining room for some seasons, and Evelyn Pearson. The Sears family had been connected to the Matthews family. I think my mother stayed with a Sears in Cincinnati when she went to school. It was Connie Mack Jr., who I had been working with at the Chamber of Commerce, who introduced me to his father.

Jimmie Foxx

Branch Rickey

This was the only time I was ever thrilled to meet a celebrity. Any other time, I was underwhelmed. Now, if I could sit down and talk to whichever celebrity I was meeting, that would be another story.

The baseball manager Branch Rickey came over and bought a cane fishing pole from me. He was a crusty old guy. He was a huge figure in baseball, elected to the Hall of Fame in 1967. He was known for breaking the color barrier for drafting Jackie Robinson, for creating the framework for the modern farm team system, and for introducing the batting helmet. But he wanted to fish with a cane pole!

All I was involved with was football, boxing, track — we didn't have any golf, baseball I was no good at — and softball (I repeat: I hate that term and I'm just going to keep saying it; that ball is anything but soft). We played sandlot softball where you never knew what position you'd play.

Throughout school, what was always in my mind was that I wanted to travel around the world but I didn't get very far. Uncle Sam knocked on my door. Three years later I got out of the Army and again thought I would travel but guess what? Zoom — right back to Sanibel I went.

DUTY CALLS: THE ARMY

I was a junior in college when the war broke out. I remember I was sitting in a Morris chair — the forerunner of the recliner — reading the funny papers and someone came in and said, "They bombed Pearl Harbor." What did I know at that time? I thought Pearl Harbor was in the Philippines — and I thought I was reasonably good in geography. You didn't think much about it right away. I can't say that I was anxious to get into combat the way young men sometimes are. One of my roommates took off and became a Navy pilot. He went MIA on his first foray and we never found out any more about it. If you go down in the middle of the Pacific Ocean, who the heck's going to know where you are?

That was in December of course. I went through the spring and we went through the next summer of 1942 and I decided I better enlist. I went over to Camp Pickett in Blackstone and enlisted and they signed me up to go in the Army in June 1943 when I was supposed to graduate — if I graduated.

I happened to be in the infirmary in January 1943 with some sort of thing. They got hold of me and asked me when my next semester ended, which was February 25 and I had to report for duty. The Army wanted me to finish whatever I was doing to get an education, but after that I just had enough time to come home for a day or so and then report to Boca Raton. That's the way it is: when you sign up, they have you. As far as they were concerned, the next day I was in the Army. I had committed myself body and soul to the U.S. Army. A few days later I was in Boca Raton, arriving around 5 or 6 in the morning. And so I found myself in the Army, during a war, on a bus on a cold February morning. That's a lonely feeling. I got off the bus in Boca and Army personnel were there to greet us, if that's what you want to call it.

I was in Virginia and I don't think they realized I was a Floridian or they would have sent me someplace else. It seemed they sent the northern boys south, and the southern boys north.

I was #13185468 now, that was my serial number. I can still recite it, almost 70 years later. I was in the Air Corps, there being no Air Force then. I started out in Boca Raton, went to Goldsboro, North Carolina; New Haven, Connecticut; Grand Rapids, Michigan; Salt Lake City, Utah; Madison, Wisconsin; Champaign - Urbana, Illinois; and ended up back where I started in Boca Raton. I was actually discharged at Camp Blanding in Stark, Florida.

I went in the Army directly as a cadet and we did not go to the ramshackle barracks I was later to reside in. We were in the Boca Raton Club, which is still in operation. Well, I should say the "former" Boca Raton Club – it was stripped for the Army to use it. It was relatively fancy, although we were eight men in a room for two, but we weren't very far from the ocean. The quarters had two pools, saltwater and freshwater. Of course, there was barely enough room to walk by the double-deck beds and the carpet had been moved, so the glue was all over the floor. It was our job to remove that glue. We put towels in front of the crack of the door and flooded the room and let it soak all night and went to bed. And that story ends there because that's all I can remember. I was in so many different barracks in so many different places. Most of the time they were tarpaper shacks.

In Grand Rapids, Michigan, we were housed in a hotel downtown next to the Convention Center that was used as classrooms. I didn't do too well in classes, so the Army decided I wasn't going to be a meteorologist. After that, I was sent to Salt Lake City Army Air Corps where I was in the Army Air base in the confines of the civilian air base, right in town. At one time they issued us full field equipment, everything except the steel helmet, and we thought we were going somewhere overseas, but a week later they took it all away from us. That's the way things work in the Army. My next stop was Camp Kearns near Salt Lake City for probably less than a month, where we were just waiting to be shipped someplace else. What a hole that place was.

We would have white glove inspections at Goldsboro and in Boca. When I was in the Cadet Corps we shined our belt buckles, which were brass 1-1/2 inch square, and the back side had to be just as shiny as the front side. Everything had to be precise and neat and clean. Did you ever hear of field stripping a cigarette? When you got down to the end of a cigarette, you would remove the paper and scatter the tobacco so there would be no butts lying around. You can't do that with a filtered cigarette. That's how neat and clean we had to be.

I also learned to drink coffee in the Army. I noticed when we had KP duty, soldiers would drink coffee on break. I didn't drink coffee, so they would put me back to work. Guess what? The next morning, Bailey was drinking coffee.

I spent some time at Yale learning to build radios before I was off to Truax Field in Madison, Wisconsin where I was going to school to learn to be a radio repairman and graduated at the top of my class. Now, radar is just another form of radio, and during the early part of the war radar was very secretive. For example, it was only many years later that I learned what happened to a soldier who might have been me, and I think radar was involved. There was a trailer containing some kind of equipment located in the middle of a big field, and it was always guarded. I was assigned to guard the trailer but at the last minute, the Corporal of the Guard changed his mind and assigned me to something else. Well, that poor guy was hurt when lightning struck nearby, and although I don't think he was killed, I was glad not to be there. I only found that out right before I was discharged. Boca was a big radio school and that's where I was assigned, but then the war ended.

My next stop was Chanute Field in Champaign-Urbana, Illinois for more radio school. I was there when Roosevelt died. I was sitting in a grounded airplane in a class where we were doing radio training when the word came. I just remember it was hard to believe. He got elected four times. People sway back and forth and I've said this for years: I don't think he would have been re-elected the second time if the election had been held in the summer. Wendell Wilke would have won. But he talked too much, as they all do sometimes. If Wilke had kept his mouth shut, he might have been president.

Shortly thereafter the war in Europe was over, May 1945, and they shipped me back to Boca Raton, right back to where I started my Army career. I didn't do too much there but a lot of guard duty. Things weren't so rushed and harried and people weren't pushing us to do anything. In fact, they were looking for jobs for us to do. What they say in the Army is, "If it moves, salute it; if it doesn't move, pick it up; if you can't pick it up, paint it."

In August the war was totally over, on both fronts, and to be discharged you had to have a certain number of points. I had too many points to be sent overseas but not enough to be discharged. I ended up in what was called "routing." Everything traveled by railroad in those days, whether it was freight or people, and routing everyone where they needed to go was my job. I had a secretary and together we routed people to their proper places.

When it came time for me to be discharged I went to Camp Blanding in Starke, Florida, not too far from Jacksonville which is the National Guard camp now, not a regular Army post. It's a big place.

When I was getting ready to be discharged, my brother John drove me up, and even though the Model T we had didn't look anywhere near as nice as it does today on display at the Sanibel Historical Museum and Village, in those days any Model T was quite a thing. The young guard on duty, his eyes were as big as saucers seeing a guy in uniform and a guy in civilian clothes in a Model T, even a beat-up one.

I knew the Army was doing some kind of testing for an atomic bomb on the island of Bikini and I came very close to signing up to go there. Thank God I didn't, not for the length of time I would spend, but for the exposure to radiation.

I had my knee operated on while I was in the Army. I could have gotten 20 percent disability because of this, but I turned it down. For one thing, it would take a week or two to get it approved, and I chose to go home instead. This was back in North Carolina. I was walking along down a little bit of a slope and my leg locked up. I couldn't straighten it and I couldn't bend it. There were two surgeons there operating on me and I heard one complaining to the other that he was taking too long and being too precise. "You're trying to match up every cell," this doctor complained, as though to tell the other surgeon to hurry and be less meticulous. I told that complaining doctor, "It's my knee, let him do it." I was able to play football after that, too.

There's been a lot of talk about the Greatest Generation, and for those who deserve that designation, I think it's great and wonderful. But I hardly did anything. I don't consider myself a war veteran. I did what I was told for three years, but it didn't amount to anything.

In some ways we were all goof-offs during our time in the Army. After I was home, I would say to myself, "Wait a minute, you're not in the Army, now get back to work!" Sometimes in the Army we simply didn't have much to do. They would get us in formation and march us off someplace to pick up trash or something. We would watch the sergeant very carefully and find a safe moment to drift off someplace and do something else.

I wanted to serve in the Army and do my part. And although I never served in the field, it takes several men behind one man in the field to put him out there. Taking nothing away from a foot soldier or an aviator, what wins a war is logistics: procurement, storage, and disbursement of uniforms, clothing, ammunition, guns, airplanes, the whole works. If you don't have that, the poor guy in the field can't do anything. Again, that takes nothing away from the valor and the patriotism of the guy out there who's being shot at.

I was discharged on George Washington's birthday in February 1946. Well, some people call it George Washington's birthday – I call it my liberation day. The Army is an experience I'm glad I had but I wouldn't want to do it again. And I had it easy compared to others.

Now, when I got out of college, I wanted to travel around the world. Just like a lot of people in their hometowns, I thought I wanted to get out of this place, out of Sanibel. I didn't have that feeling as strong as my brothers Sam and John did; they were interested in things that weren't available on Sanibel. I did make a bluff at playing various sports, but bluff is about all you could call it. I saw myself going to Alaska, South America – don't ask me why. I've been there two or three times since. But after the war I found I wanted to go home, and home I went.

TEACHER AND CAMP COUNSELOR

Back on Sanibel, I worked for Daddy, played softball, and was at my wit's end – I still had itchy feet. In the summer of 1946 all three Bailey brothers were here for a while and then Sam had to report to football camp in Hershey, Pennsylvania for pre-season. I was still floundering around even then, so I decided to go see my Uncle Clark in Lewistown, Pennsylvania, and hitchhiked there with Sam. After two or three days of hitchhiking, we would be sitting in the road for hours sometimes and we would pitch pennies and talk. After a couple of days we didn't get very far so we finally split up – it's easier to catch a ride if you're alone – and sure enough I got a ride. I can't remember what Sam did to get to Hershey, but I got to Lewistown.

Everybody hitchhiked back then. In fact, hitchhiking was my only transportation in college. The college was five miles south of the little town of Farmville. There was a corner on the campus where cars went through and you'd just stand there and someone would stop – country people, professors – and we would take turns catching a ride, in order.

> **...we would be sitting in the road for hours sometimes and we would pitch pennies and talk.**

I'm not sure what made me go up to Uncle Clark's. I liked my uncle and he had helped me in school; he got me an interview with a radio station in Gainesville to be an announcer. It was one of the shocks of my life to listen to my own voice, and I hated it. I did not take that job.

I had one more year of eligibility in football, which I really liked, and there were some classes I wanted to take in math, particularly The Theory of Equations. The dean said, "You don't want to come here; you have your degree. Why don't you teach school? You don't need a special teaching degree to teach in a prep school," and the school I graduated from was looking for teachers, and they knew me. I didn't have anything else in mind. I hadn't settled down enough to know I wanted to work at Daddy's store. I liked it, but was that what I wanted to do? I didn't know yet. The school hired me and off I went back to Hampton Sydney in Lynchburg.

When I was teaching school, I was always "Mr. Bailey." Maybe the headmaster, if we were totally alone, would call me Francis. That's how it was then. We called Daddy's secretary Miss Lula, and Clarence Rutland's wife Miss Ruth.

It was while I was home on Christmas vacation from teaching school that I met Mr. Starry. The island was still pretty dead, but there was a man and his wife at the Island Inn named Starry and he had a boy's camp in Ely, Vermont named Camp Passumpsic, and he offered me a job being a counselor. I didn't know what it was all about, but I decided to try it anyway.

I still have the contracts hiring me to work at Camp Passumpsic in 1947. For the period from June 28 through August 27, my compensation was $175, plus a $25 bonus for "completing a nice job." It eventually went up to $200, plus a $25 commission for each new member enrolled for the next season.

I worked primarily with land sports in the camp, teaching baseball, football, tag, things like that. There were no frills at the camp – no windows, just shutters that came up – but we didn't need any frills. As counselors we used to get up early sometimes on Sunday mornings and ride horses but those horses didn't like me! I'm not much of a horseman.

Before camp opened, being a counselor meant you were also a laborer. One of the chores we had to accomplish was putting a dock out in the lake. We worked in just bathing trunks, so from the waist up we would be sunburned and our bottoms would be white as a sheet of paper, or blue from the cold! That was on Lake Fairlee, Vermont, not quite across the state line from Dartmouth in New Hampshire. Later on in life, when I worked at Bailey's store, my "uniform" was a white tee shirt and long pants – not much better for getting an even tan.

When it came time for swimming all of us went down to the docks and we were all lifeguards – and to the camp, "lifeguard" meant "keep your eyes on the kids." We didn't have any qualifications but we would watch the kids. We used the buddy system. If they blew the whistle, which they did arbitrarily, and the children didn't match up with their buddies right quick, you were out. That's a method

On the left; as a camp counselor I was charged with lifeguard duty. Here we're starting a race.

used in lots of different places. The biggest thing we got out of that was teaching a couple of kids how to swim.

One child I particularly remember was the son of the publisher of National Geographic magazine. I don't think that boy had ever been in anything bigger than a bathtub. Let's just say he was no Michael Phelps (or in my day we would have said he was no Johnny Weissmuller), but we taught him to swim and that was very rewarding.

Counselors taught fitness, baseball and football.

I came to realize I didn't have enough patience to teach school, but I taught algebra and it was gratifying. There was a little boy who couldn't get it the first period and I worked and worked with him and he earned a passing grade. It's the noblest thing – a warm, satisfying feeling.

Another student from Texas used to sit in the back of the room and throw spitballs. I would have liked to give a test to catch him unawares and teach him a lesson about paying attention, but then most of the rest of the class would have failed and that didn't seem fair.

I taught school another year, and camp another year before deciding school teaching definitely was not for me even though they wanted me to come back. I went to Richmond, Virginia, where my second-cousin-once-removed lived and got a job in a lumber yard as a shipping clerk. I lived at the corner of Grove and Allen with my cousin Lillian, Mrs. Crawford, in her house. I was only there from about September to December, but that's where I learned some of the lingo of the building trade.

It was there in Richmond, by the way, that I played my last of football and switched over to softball, which I would continue to play into my 80s.

It was sometime in December I decided the grass was not quite as green there as I thought it was, so I went home. I found myself missing the smell of sea water. I've never been much of a fisherman, but that smell reminded me of home. At Christmas I'd hear Bing Crosby singing White Christmas and I was not dreaming of a white Christmas — I was dreaming of white sandy beaches. .

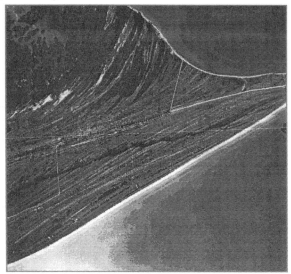
One of Sanibel's white sandy beaches from the air around 1947

BACK TO SANIBEL

Sanibel almost died during World War II. All the young people were in the service. Clarence Rutland was a fireman at Page Field. There was still some activity, though. When I was stationed over at Boca Raton the last eight or nine months that I was in the service, I used to get leave and come home on weekends once in a while. And there just wasn't anybody here.

I was on the island for two weeks in 1944 on furlough, and then got an extra two weeks to help clean up after the hurricane. That was a devastating storm. Gusts topped 160 mph, with sustained winds of 120 mph. It left $10 million in damage ($107 million in 2005 US dollars). It is estimated that if a similar hurricane struck here in the year 2005, it would cause $38.7 billion in damage, making it one of the worst-case storms for western Florida.

Normally there's a lot of rain before, during and after a hurricane. But it was one of the worst droughts ever in 1944. It was always dry, and my father was always worried about that. I remember years before after a good rain when Mother was still alive, Daddy came back with a handful of absolutely dusty soil one day and showed it to Mother. Mother said something like, "Farmers are never satisfied."

There was not a lot of rain during the hurricane of that year – actually, we never called them hurricanes then, we called them storms. It left a lot of minerals and salt in the soil, and it takes a lot of washing to get rid of it. The salt water went right down into the

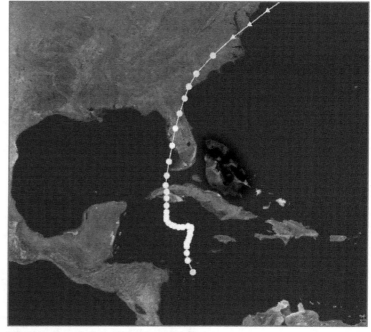

The path of the 1944 hurricane

earth. Water and earth are pretty wonderful things, what they do, but it takes time for salt water to leach out of the ground.

We got warnings about that storm over the Western Union telegraph. Everybody had a barometer and during hurricane season, you lived by it. There are signs of weather anyway, if you're outdoors all the time the way many of us were. You can see things.

The water didn't quite get in our house but it came up so high Daddy thought it was going to. During the eye of the storm, which passed right over Sanibel, Daddy and Martin Hiers (Allen Nave's step-daddy) went outside and when they went back in, the water started coming up fast. The eye is a distinct calm and if you hadn't had the experience, you would think it's all over, and that's how people get killed sometimes. And then the wind changes direction. Daddy was in the house with Martin Hiers and Allen Nave and it got to the point where they decided to take all the books out of the bottom shelf of the bookcase. Daddy told me he was thinking, "We may not make it, but it's as good a way as any to go." Daddy was not the kind of person who was easily frightened, but he thought that this was the end.

Things changed after that storm. It used to be a person could dig a well six or seven feet and get good fresh water. It was hard water, but it was fresh and you could put it on a seed bed. If you put a barrel down your well and left it alone, it would keep the sand from coming in. We put down Coca Cola barrels like open-ended cylinders. Still, there was always a certain amount of sand that would get in no matter what you did.

In 1946, I was out of the Army and working at the store, and John and I were on a softball team sponsored by Bartley's Sporting Goods Store. We were the city champions that year. Then, after not playing for many years – I was married and taking care of the store and had children to consider – I did take up softball again. I played softball for a long time, off-island for a number of years, in North Fort Myers, in Cape Coral next to the hospital, then on Sanibel in a league that we formed in the 1970s. I have a lot of good memories related to softball. There was a standing joke between Sam and John about my softball skills. They would put me in right field because it was the least dangerous spot. One time, as Sam told it, "Francis was playing center field, and someone hit a fly ball to him. He came rushing in, looked up, and the ball was behind him. He moved back, and the ball hit right where he was standing. He picked up the ball and threw it right over the backstop."

> **We could have had a triple play except everybody was just doubled up laughing.**

Sam and John were right about my abilities. During one game in North Fort Myers I was playing left field. Allen Nave was in charge at the time and playing center field. Someone hit the ball in my direction. I looked up to catch it and all I could see was lights. About that time the ball hit me in the head, bounced over to Allen Nave, who caught it and threw it to second for an out. We could have had a triple play except everybody was just doubled up laughing. But I got an assist on the play anyway.

I was not very good at softball, obviously, and they used to tease me as they were choosing up nine people that I was their tenth choice. In desperation they usually put me in right field. When they have a player they don't know what to do with, they put him in right field. I wasn't very good at it, but I sure did enjoy it. One of the sad times of my life was when I had to quit playing at age 79. I really, really enjoyed playing. Various and sundry things contributed to my having to quit.

CHAPTER 4
MY LIFE AS SANIBEL'S STOREKEEPER

SANIBEL PACKING COMPANY/BAILEY'S GENERAL STORE

I came back to Sanibel for good in December 1948 when I was 27 and worked for Daddy. I always felt, and so did my brothers, that Sanibel was home, in spite of our youthful desires to see the world. We came home whenever we wanted to but Daddy had his rules when we were home, and they were very fair rules. The welcome mat was big and open and it always was and always would be, not like today. At 27, I was still part of the household at the homestead; it was home.

Andy Rosse's dock

Daddy bought the store from John Geraty in 1899. At that time the store was at the end of Jane Matthews' dock (no relation to Mother's family). It was destroyed in the hurricane of 1926 and Daddy built a second store and dock roughly 700 to 800 feet north (the dock pointed northeast) of Matthews, and that's where the store was located, onshore, for the next 39 years until 1966 when we moved to our present location at the corner of Periwinkle Way and Tarpon Bay Road. We've been at our current spot now longer than any other location.

Daddy was having financial troubles in the late 1940s, no ifs, ands, or buts about it — troubles brought on by the war, the Depression, and the whole place just changing. There he was up in his 70s, and it was getting to be too much for him. He was talking to people about selling the store when it was still on the bay down Bailey Road.

Daddy might have had to sell the store if I hadn't come back. John was a cowboy — well, that's what I call it but it's not exactly accurate; he was a rancher by trade – and Sam was playing

The store in its second location after a hurricane destroyed the fruit

professional football and other sports. But I really wanted to work for Daddy. I'd gotten over wanting to be a farmer — it was too much work; it's bad enough in the business I'm

The store where it ihas been since 1966, the corner of Periwinkle Way and Tarpon Bay Road

in. And I didn't want to teach. I had visions of heading out west and all these wheat fields, but I always leaned toward the retail business. I was going to raise pigeons at one time. I was going to sell school supplies at one time. Daddy stopped me on that: there were less than 30 people in the school (this was before 1935) and most of them were poor as church mice. No, what I wanted was to work in the store and take over for Daddy. I missed what was here. I wasn't exactly an ambitious one. And in part I thought I should. You do have some obligation to your parents, and I had no particular career plan like my two brothers did.

Selling anything, even your own services, is all basically the same. You're offering somebody a service that they need or want and you have to satisfy your customer. That's the backbone of any decent business: service. Sometimes it's a little difficult to satisfy everybody but you can try. Some people you're never going to satisfy: they complain if the sun comes up in the morning, they complain if it's cloudy.

My brothers and I had always worked in the store and it was pretty primitive in those days. When we started out there was just a big long counter. I was on one side as a clerk; the customer would tell me what he wanted and I would get it for him. If you wanted a can of peaches, I'd get the peaches – then if you wanted a can of peas, I would go back to the same spot and get the can of peas. People did wander around and browse, we certainly didn't prevent that. Then I would write it up, item by item.

One time when Uncle Harry was still here, he was weighing out some sugar or whatever using the balance scale, with the appropriate weight on

Pauline, my first wife, and I opening the store in the mid-1950s

110

one side while he filled the customer's sack on the other side – well, nobody bought a pound of anything and you would think that surely Uncle Harry would notice he was filling the bag too full. It turned out every time he leaned over, someone was adding a little more weight to the scale, and the next thing you know the sugar or whatever item it was would be spilling all over the floor.

At least that's the way I heard the story. The scale never balanced because some smart aleck guys were horsing around and Uncle Harry didn't notice. Uncle Harry never worked in the store in my lifetime; he didn't even live on the island then.

In the old days, serving the customer the way we did, fetching their items, was necessary. They wouldn't have known where anything was anyway. Maybe it wasn't always quite that slow, but that's the way it worked. We had 100-pound sacks of flour, not just little packages; people did more baking then. There were 55-gallon drums of relatively light metal that Daddy had painted white filled with sugar, grits, and all kinds of beans – lima, northern, navy, black-eyed peas. There was no packaging. Some of the horse feed came in 200-pound sacks. We had salt-cured slab bacon, sometimes quite thick. That type of merchandise doesn't lend itself to shopping for different brands or other options.

Sam had introduced some paint to our stock. Gradually I put in new refrigerated equipment and added some frozen food. Prior to that all we had were two small refrigerators, like people's home refrigerators, for customers' milk and for perishables, in case someone didn't pick them up right away, plus we would get a little extra. We sold cheese by the pound. We used to cut slices for customers from big round wheels. You would get so good slicing the exact weight they wanted, you would get mad at yourself if you were a quarter-ounce off.

The store as it operated at the end of Bailey Road, from 1926 to 1966.

We wrote slips for each customer and did much of our business on credit.

The number of perishable items was almost nil, though. We stocked very little; mostly we had standing orders for those things. Prior to those refrigerators, there were iceboxes. Purchases were wrapped in paper. At each end of the counter was paper and a cone of string. It was very light thread – you could break it with your hand. And nearly everybody had a charge account – we used very little cash.

People didn't really look around the way they do today, or at least not as much. They didn't come in with big shopping lists, and I'm not even sure when shopping carts came along. The transition to the way it is today was a slow one.

Ledgers were kept daily for each shopper. We wrote up little charge slips with three copies. The top two had carbons underneath, and the bottom one was pink. The customer got the pink one with the product. One copy was sent out with the bills at the end of the month, and the other one was a permanent thing we kept.

Not many new products introduced, where today there's something new every 15 minutes – that's not right, it's every 15 seconds. One thing Daddy introduced was canvas shoes similar to Keds; in fact, Keds was our competition. The canvas shoes were made overseas, and we'd order in the summer and get them in the winter. We ordered from samples. The salesman would come in late spring/early summer with samples; the shoes weren't even made yet. The manufacturer would poke a hole in the sample shoes – mid-sole, about the size of a pencil – so as not to pay duty on them. We always had to beg and plead to get the order in November, and sometimes we did. With shoes, of course people had to try them on.

Our clothing store — a bit crowded

We sold some clothing, but there was no dressing room. For the size of the store, we sold quite a lot of women's shorts and blouses. Our customers were primarily people who didn't bring proper clothing from the north.

All our groceries were marked individually with a tag or with the price written right on them. That changed, too, with prices now on the shelves. I thought that change would create an uproar of protest, but it never did. Of course in the grocery business, cleanliness is important, and it was back then as well. It wasn't always easy to know what to stock, though. For example, we couldn't keep Noxzema on the shelves. There's a story that a guy goes into a little country store and almost the entire store is filled with salt. He says, "You must sell a lot of salt!" and the store owner answers, "No, but the salt salesman does!"

Daddy told me one time that since I started working there it was the first time since his bookkeeper left that all the posting was done. Uncle Ernest was supposed to do it but didn't do too well. The ledgers are still in the Bailey's General Store offices today. In the ones from the 1940s, you can see entries for bread for 16 cents, and for Lysol for the Island Inn for 30 cents.

THE GAS STATION

The Tea Room by the store's parking lot on the bay was built to serve as a gas station but that didn't work out and we moved it across from the ferry landing where it later became Miss Charlotta's Tea Room. There Daddy built a nine-hole miniature golf course behind it, between the store and the Tea Room. The last time I remember seeing it there is 1935. I played it some. The course had archways, an overpass bridge, the greens were treated cotton seed, and you would tee off from a rock structure that had cement on the top of it. The rocks were coquina rock, and there's still a little bit of the wall left. It was not much of a success.

The Tea Room in its heyday

The Tea Room served as the temporary store after the 1926 hurricane, then between 1928 and 1935 it became Miss Charlotta's Tea Room and lastly, a private residence primarily for people who worked in the store until it was moved to the museum in 1993 or '94. No gas was ever sold out of the Tea Room although the structure was built to accommodate a gas station. It was just an idea that didn't work out because the store was washed away and Daddy needed the Tea Room as a temporary store. When they built the store on the bay they put an overhang to accommodate two gas pumps and so the Tea Room wasn't necessary for use as a gas station. The ferry moved away from that dock in 1937 or '38, and that was about it.

Sam and I used to love to pump the gas when we were little. Daddy must have lost a fortune in the fumes. But

The Tea Room today , restored at the Sanibel Historical Museum and Village

we had the gas pumps at the store for 28 years, since 1927. Before that there was a fuel pump at the end of the Matthews dock in the early 1920s or teens. Some of the northern people shipped cars down here and I don't know what they did for gasoline. Once Daddy asked one of them what a tire cost and he answered, "If you have to ask, you have no business owning a car."

Business and activity were spreading out as early as the 1950s. The post office was on Reed's Landing – prior to that, Mrs. Nutt was postmaster, most likely in her house. Reed's Landing is where Mother arrived on the island and thought the fiddler crabs were spiders, and there was a vacant hotel down there when I came along. That's where the action was at first, before Bailey's, but you could read the writing on the wall. We were going to be on a dead-end street. We figured we could do better by having a full-fledged gas station, so we built one in 1956; it was Standard Oil of Kentucky at the time. It was called Sanibel Service Station, now the BP station. We operated it ourselves at first, or really I did. Sam wasn't here at all. I worked up there one or two days, filling in for people. Later we leased it to people and eventually sold it to Jim Anholt.

Every night after supper I would go down to the station, take the money out, count it, and turn off all the lights. You never left a night light on. I remember I would look toward the lighthouse. No matter where you looked, it was absolute darkness and that was even after the island had started to develop some. One time just where the shopping center Periwinkle Place is now, about a half-mile walk from the gas station, I pulled the car by the side of the road. I left the keys in it of course, and there were absolutely no lights anywhere in those days before the bridge.

I never took the keys out of the ignition, in fact, not even in Fort Myers. Now every time I get out of the car I lock it. One of the reasons is habit. But another is this: One time my wife June and I had one of our two dogs in my car and one in June's car. June shut the door and left the motor running, and this little beast stepped on the lock and locked it. We did everything imaginable to somehow encourage the little beast to unlock it. We finally called roadside service and they didn't do anything; they said leave it running until the gas runs out. We ended up breaking a window. So much for roadside service.

Anyway, there were no houses from the gas station to just before the lighthouse, and the only houses down there were the lighthouse keeper's house and the lighthouse itself. With no artificial lights on, you can still see quite a bit, though. It never gets completely dark like it does when you get in a closet. I like a brilliant full moon on a clear night, there's nothing like it. Oh, it's gorgeous.

THE MODERNIZATION OF BAILEY'S GENERAL STORE

Daddy had been plugging along at the store, trying to take care of his brother and the three wild Indians that were his boys, and no wife. Daddy was 75 when I came back. Your approach to life changes at that age. People owed him a lot of money. One of his favorite sayings was he could get along with raggedy overalls and eat beans but he wanted better for his boys.

I'm sure he was glad when I came back and the store could remain Bailey's. We weren't always very effusive in my family, but I think he was proud of me – he was proud of all his sons; we had different accomplishments.

Daddy and I made improvements at the store along the way. Just before Daddy died we built a 14-foot extension on the back and built a walk-in insulated cooler. We were not quite finished when he died in 1952.

I remember Daddy's desk was always messy with lots of ink spots on it. There was no such thing as a ballpoint pen or even a fountain pen. The cat always knocked his ink well all over everything. As messy as it may have gotten, though, Daddy always knew exactly where everything was and he was very efficient. He never had perfect eyesight, and because of that he needed bright light at his desk and had to use pencils with thick lead, which makes it hard to write small. Esperanza said it like it was: "How come you can see all these girls with their pretty legs but you can't see that?" I'm like my father, I need lots of light to see and I use the same thick-leaded pencils.

I always had a cat in the store with me.

A number of years went along. My best and first secretary, in spite of the fact that I have had some excellent ones since then, grew up on the island and lived next door to us for a while. Her name was Grace Rhodes. She would come out in fancy bloomers so we started calling her Dorothy Lamour. I always had a cat in the store with me, and I continued that when the store moved to its current location, where Miss B lived in the office for 15 years. In earlier days, cats were allowed in the store, but Miss B was never in the store. In fact, she wouldn't go out the door. She would think she was going to the vet; she didn't know what the vet was, she just knew it was a horrible experience.

Since those days, a world of complications have grown up with the business, as well as with the island – more and more over the years. Some things have gotten easier — the self-serve at the store, for example. No one asks for a can of peaches anymore and I don't have to get them anymore.

I got some valuable lessons from Daddy in salesmanship, and not necessarily just groceries. For example, something would be selling in the clothing or hardware sections – pocket knives or sunglasses – but not selling all that much and I'd

I continue in the tradition of Daddy's messy desk.

say, "We don't need to order that anymore." He'd answer that people don't buy things from an empty shelf, they buy them from a display. It can't look leftover or old. So we'd change things around and they would start to sell. We only had one or two areas like that in those days, and they did get kind of dusty and neglected once in a while. But the items had sold in the past and probably would sell again. Buying anything in the retail business is a gamble. People's buying habits change radically many times. But you stuck to the same principles back then as you do today.

We just worked along and tried to do things that hadn't been done for a long time. It became kind of routine after a while. People ask me my least favorite job at the store and I always answer, "Work!" but I remember hauling plenty of ice to put in people's refrigerators, and those five-gallon glass bottles of water that I used to pick up one in each hand and just walk off with them. That's beyond an impossibility for me now!

One of the advantages of Bailey's being independent of a chain was we could just do what we thought best, whether it was moving the store, putting product where we wanted to – we just did it. Without a chain, though, you don't have the same buying power, so there are advantages and disadvantages. As an independent, you have a better chance sometimes to provide the consumers with what they want rather than what some guy in a swivel chair thinks they want or what the manufacturer has slammed down their throats.

That's why we belong to a cooperative, or co-op. The theory is that if two grocers both need a half case of something, they can join forces, split it, and save money. Otherwise suppliers can't deliver because there's no way to pay for the truck. The co-op is a wholesaler; they can be your warehouse so you can buy in greater quantities.

We have two co-ops on the island: Island Water Association, and the Lee County Electric Cooperative. If you pay for water, you're a member of IWA – you're a part owner. That kind of cooperative is a little bit different than the grocery cooperative. They get pretty big sometimes, even though they start out small. Also, if your store has a particular competitor, you have to watch out and make sure you don't get in the same cooperative.

Most of the business was a charge business, which was deadly. In terms of economics, every time you carry an account, the value of it goes down considerably. Your money works for you when you have it, not when you don't have it.

Three or four years ago, I went with my son-in-law Richard Johnson to a seminar. Richard manages the store now – in fact, he and my daughter own the store, but I can't tell the difference. At that seminar, they had us work out the arithmetic to show what waiting 30 days for payment does to your cash flow. Extending credit is a practice that continues today. It's becoming sort of a status thing to have an account at Bailey's. We don't solicit them but if someone asks – well, it's like a slap in the face if you turn them down.

Daddy, though, extended credit for the sake of the island. A farmer doesn't have the money and needs things, and at the end of the season he's going to pay you. If he doesn't make any money or if he's slovenly, then you're out of luck.

The way I learned the business could be called baptism under fire. I made a lot of mistakes along the way and still make some. You try not to make the same ones over again. I worked seven days a week and still do. I was away from home a lot with the business when the children were growing up. That's one of the regrets I have.

One thing I learned is you can't carry everything in the store, it's just impossible. Even huge stores don't have everything. A knowledgeable man once told me if you satisfy what everybody wants you'll go broke – you simply can't stock that much stuff. You have to stay on the job and vigilantly tend to what the customers want. When people request us to stock things, we have to consider: are they permanent residents or just passing through? Is it just a whim or is it something they'll buy all the time?

Me with my children.
From left: Patrick, Susan, Mary Mead and Anne (Jane was not born yet.)

Price is important but it's not necessarily the most important factor – quality is. One thing that's an absolute given is you have to sell for more than it cost you or you won't be there to take care of your customers. And it's up to you to take care of your customers.

Some costs you can control. If you can work with people, you get along. If you're pleasant and help people, see what you can do for them and do your best, they will put up with some of your idiosyncrasies.

People sometimes ask how we know how much to order. The answer is, we don't. It's a wild guess. Of course, in the position we're in now, we have history behind us. You talk to your wholesalers and they help for the most part – tell us what's selling, what's not. You introduce new products and they fall flat on their face. I can't quote the figures on them but they're astronomical, the number of new products that come on the market and the teeny percentage of them that ever make it – and not just grocery products.

Every now and then somebody hits on something – take cereal. How many kinds there are: Corn Flakes with peanuts, with frosting, with fruit, with petunia buds – anything has a chance of making it as long as you advertise on television. New products we never even thought were possible have come out since I started. We used to just have flour. Now we have cake flour, self-rising flour, wheat flour, rye flour; plus cake mixes, biscuit mixes, plus how many different flavors and how many different brands of all those same things? And frosting to go with them. Creamers, flavored creamers, Hamburger Helper – none of that was around when I started in this business. Cigarettes, you had six or seven brands; now you don't just have Lucky Strike but you have them in long, short, soft pack, hard pack, menthol, and people want what they want and unless they're desperate, they won't buy the other one.

With the multitude of products and additional ones coming on, there's always a contest for shelf space. We don't have an exact delineation of where Brand X puts its product. Therefore, the line of demarcation can fluctuate. Nothing makes me madder than having a salesman push another company's product behind theirs or, even worse, damage the other guy's product. I won't have it.

We didn't even have frozen food. People would order meat. Milk and bread, white or wheat, were always on order, plus we would order a little extra. It wasn't as hard to keep track of as it might seem because there weren't that many items, or that many people, and there weren't all of the other complications you have today: a deli, a bakery, prepared foods. You just try to keep up with things. Now we've added a deli, bakery, meat market and coffee bar at the store.

Today there's a bit of a trend toward self-checkouts. I don't know exactly how it works, but I know some people don't want to do that. One woman told me years ago when we changed to a more modern cash register — the type where for 43 cents you would push down the 40 and then push down the 3 and flags came up "43 cents" and that was supposed to be real fancy — and the woman was furious. "You bought a new machine so you could raise your prices and charge me more!" She was a very nice lady but, boy, she didn't like that. I tried to explain it would make it easier and quicker, but it did no good.

I do believe that employees are the backbone of a business. A lot of former employees from years ago come back and tell me they enjoyed working here, and that is gratifying.

What we look for most in employees is loyalty and willingness to learn. It was so hard getting people when the ferry didn't run that often. If we got somebody to work, I would ask them to at least promise to stay to the end of the season. And as far as I am concerned if they behaved themselves, they had a job here. We don't have as many problems today because jobs are hard to find – and we have a bridge. Sometimes people working for other stores come here. Often, particularly the younger ones, they think they want to work here and then their girlfriend moves away or they get a better offer and they're gone – sometimes with no notice, no phone call.

Now potential employees have to drive by a lot of other stores that might offer them employment before they come across the bridge and that makes it hard to get people, so we try to keep a pleasant environment so people want to work here. One of the things we do to make it attractive to work at the store is pay for employees' tolls.

Of course, if you have no customers, you can't pay your employees. So sometimes, it's a circular question who is more important, employees or customers. It's also difficult to see if you have a bad employee. People who are stealing whatever particular thing it happens to be – and there haven't been too many – you just have to get rid of immediately. They may be

thinking, "I only stole a pencil," or "I only ate a sandwich." That's not good. Stealing is stealing – and when I get mad, I get mad. If I get mad enough to fire someone, watch out.

A lot of advancements made work easier for our employees. The first time I saw the UPC codes I said, "We've got to have that – but let's wait until the big boys get the bugs out of it and the price goes down." And ordering was altogether different after that.

Richard Johnson came in 2004. He was in Jacksonville and married my daughter Mary Mead in October of 1983. He was and is very capable. My other sons-in-law took different directions in life that didn't include the store.

My son-in-law Richard Johnson arrived in 2004 to help after Hurricane Charley and never left.

Richard was working for State Farm as a business consultant and that took him to Bloomington, Illinois, to the home office. His assignment there was supposed to be for two to five years – I don't know the dates – but he stayed there longer than he thought he was going to. When he came back, I brought him down to Sanibel during the summer to look at some of our computers to see whether he could help us out with that and get a feel for things.

Then when Hurricane Charley came along, Richard just packed up his tools and headed to Sanibel. I didn't ask him, but he came.

My son-in-law Mike Ward, who is married to my daughter Jane, works for U.S. Fish & Wildlife, and he put Richard's stuff in his truck so he could get back onto the island

Me, John and Sam

after Charley. He was a great help. Charley turned everything topsy-turvy. Luckily we had practically no damage to the buildings in Bailey's Center. We had no electricity at first, but it was restored relatively soon. I attribute that to the fact that there were no big trees coming down on Sanibel-Captiva Road to cut off the power. Also, the power company naturally tries to get places like hospitals back on first and while we aren't a hospital, certainly, we were a hub of people. We were open the next morning at 7 o'clock and Sam was at the front door taking care of people.

Maybe over the years there were some times I wished I had my brothers' help with the store, but my brothers let me do pretty much what I wanted. They never questioned anything I did. You can't run a store playing football in Tampa or chasing cows in Jacksonville. In later life Sam was always saying we could never agree on anything and in fact disagreed on everything – except money. We never had any arguments about money. We tried to be fair with each other.

For a time, I thought I might have to sell the store, just like my Daddy worried about that before me. Sam made the statement one time that if I passed away first – as we both expected I would, me being older – he'd sell the store and leave. He was more adamant about selling than I was. We had several offers. He said he wouldn't sell to any chain but Publix, and

Sam and I

My brother John and I

he was adamant about keeping the Bailey name and the general business the same. Then Richard came down and Sam and I were both delighted, and I think the community of Sanibel is as well. When he got here, Richard didn't know a can of peas from a pound of potatoes, but he knew people and he knew management. If he hadn't come, we would have had to sell the store, that's all. There's no use in crying over spilt milk – if you have to do it, you do it and you just get on with life.

There have been high moments and low moments running the store. Everybody has a certain tendency to forget the bad and embellish the good as time goes on. I don't think it's done deliberately. I try not to dwell on the past. One of the great moments certainly was when we finished the extension. It was two-thirds done when Daddy passed away. It was another great moment when we moved to the corner of Periwinkle Way and Tarpon Bay and then made two or three extensions after that. There were a lot of good times.

I don't know whether I'm good at this business, but I know I could be a lot better. A lot of things I did in life were pretty drab, though. Sam was much more colorful, or even John.

Since its earliest days and in part because it's operated consistently and continuously, I do believe the Bailey's store has been one of the backbones of Sanibel. We've tried to be more than a store but also an involved and caring part of the community. In the early days of Sanibel, without

Bailey's - Growing since 1899

I do believe Bailey's store has been one of the backbones of Sanibel.

Daddy the island probably couldn't have grown. That's almost certainly true. And I'm happy that I was able to step in so Daddy didn't have to sell the store, and that my son-in-law Richard came along to carry on the tradition.

I don't know how Daddy would have felt if the store had been sold when he couldn't carry on any longer. I'm not sure he felt quite the same way I felt, quite as attached to it. I grew up with the store, he didn't; he was busy with other things in Kentucky – working as a shipping clerk in a steel mill. You have to do what you have to do, and if selling the store had become a necessity, I suspect he would have faced up to it like the

Sam liked to write poetry and he honored me on my 80th birthday.

man he was. Maybe it's like me selling our homestead – fortunately to an organization that is going to preserve it. I could have gotten a lot more money for it, but money isn't everything – although it helps sometimes. It's a bittersweet feeling – it's a relief, but at the same time it isn't a relief. Maybe that's how Daddy would have felt about the store.

On my 80th birthday, Sam presented me with a poem that still hangs in the store's offices:

> *Here's to Francis, he's true blue*
> *A solid Sanibelite citizen through and through*
> *A little wrinkled and overweight*
> *But when needed will step to the plate*
> *He's gone through 80 and maybe forever*
> *For I'm sure leaving his office chair? – Never*
> *Here's to our leader, may he always keep that seat*
> *Through winter cold and summer heat*
> *So drink your toast and let's be his fan*
> *For this is his day and he is our man*

I guess Sam knew something I didn't, because I'm still in that desk chair at least six days a week, more than 10 years later! And I love every minute of it.

THE LITTLE GIRL WITH THE BIG BOW

The store has been a very big part of my life, definitely. Sometimes maybe too big, because nothing is more important to me than my family, which started with my first wife Pauline – the little girl with the big bow – who was about four years younger than I. When I was in eighth grade, she was in fourth grade, a bit younger than Sam. Sam went three more years to school on Sanibel than I did and of course knew Pauline; so did my brother John.

Pauline Bailey, "the little girl with the big bow"

During the war, Pauline's father became a machinist working for the war effort, so she and her family weren't down here much at all; they lived in Ohio. Their last name was Engle, but it had been Englekaufer or something similar; her father shortened it after somebody called him Puddlykaufer.

Her father was a truck farmer so he didn't have work in the winter; that's how they could come here. Eventually they purchased Twin Palm on Captiva and moved down here lock, stock and barrel; in fact, he planted the twin palm that is so well-known today at Jensen's and that the Cottages and Marina are named after.

I didn't know exactly where she lived when we were going to school, though – Captiva was like a foreign country to us back then – and I was a hotshot eighth grader so why would I care where a fourth grader lived?

At that age when someone is four years younger, particularly with girls, boys have a "don't bother me" attitude. The one thing I remember about Pauline then was how cute she was and the big red ribbon in her hair; it was just so big. When Pauline went to high school, she didn't come down in the winters anymore. And because she was a dancer and was in a show of Frank Sinatra's, she didn't come down right away when her family moved here permanently.

I didn't lay eyes on her again after I left for school in 1939 until I got back in December 1948. Girls were scarce on the island in those days, and Sam was rounding up girls for a party on Christmas Eve after the ceremony at church. We young people were full of vinegar. Pauline was living here at that time and she

Winter 1949 at Twin Palm

124

was working at 'Tween Waters for Mrs. Grace Price. We went to my first cousin Sam Matthews' place where he was renting (he was down here on his honeymoon). I took Pauline home to her parents' home on Captiva, Twin Palm, and that was the end of it — she had her tenterhooks in me.

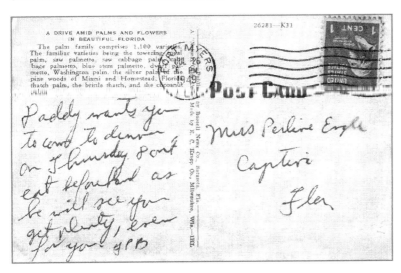

When we were courting, I used to send her postcards up in Captiva, where the post master, Beulah Wiles, was known to read people's postcards. So whenever I sent one I would put right in the middle of it, "Hi, Beulah." There were no phones between Sanibel and Captiva so the only way to communicate would be to go there or through the mail. Every now and then I would send something to Pauline up there.

We had five children, all adopted except the last one, Jane. Anne was born October 3, 1956; Susan on January 20, 1958; Mary Mead on May 9, 1961; Patrick on June 25, 1962; and Jane on May 9, 1964.

Pauline was a professional dancer. Back before Frank Sinatra was popular, she was in some programs with him. There was a dance she did one time where she had to go on stage barefoot with some doves and the doves pooped. She was meticulous about washing her feet, yet she was the only one who got plantar warts from it. This was all before I got involved with her.

In Havana, 1951

We got married in April of 1951. Pauline's mother told us, "Pauline can't move back home but Francis is welcome." She was teasing, of course. We spent our honeymoon in Havana, Cuba.

I admit I wasn't making much noise about moving out of the homestead. Daddy said, "You're not living here with me; you can visit, but you're not living here." Mike Billhimer's grandfather Clint Sears had built Hi Tide on West Gulf Drive. Next door was By the Sea.

On the Prado, Havana, April 1951

Our little house on the gulf

After we got married, Daddy divided some land he had on the gulf among the three boys. This was property he gave to Mother in 1935 when he was afraid he was going to lose it. It went to the three of us when she died, but as far as our family was concerned, Daddy owned it. Over the years, he sold a few lots here and there. Sam and I each got two and a half lots next to each other, and John got three lots because there was a pond on the property interfering with what he could use. Pauline and I stayed at the Island Inn and then in Hi Tide all summer while building our house on my lot, which had 250 feet of gulf front. Our new little house had a living room, kitchen, and bathroom with the ability to expand it. Daddy and Uncle Ernest remained in the homestead until their deaths.

Many years later that piece of property on the gulf was worth a lot of money and I didn't want it. At one time I needed to take care of the kids' schooling, but I didn't anymore. A valuable piece of property can become a drain on your pocketbook so I wanted to sell it.

Pauline, 1947

We were happy at our beach house.

The beach house was a very well-built house. This was after the city was formed. In those days some of the rules were laid out so that you were afraid to set a precedent, so it wasn't moved at that time. Sam decided he wanted to move it onto his adjacent property so he could have the house. So now the house is on his property, on West Gulf Drive just west of Tarpon Bay Road.

Pauline and me

THE BAILEY BROTHERS GET MARRIED

My brothers and I all got married around the same time – seems the Bailey men marry a bit later in life than the average; Daddy was 46, I was 30, John 28, and Sam 27. So the generations in the Bailey family are kind of stretched out. Three generations, instead of spanning 75 years, are going to come closer to spanning 175 years. Most assume that a generation is about 25 years but ours are closer to 50.

Pauline and me on our wedding day, April 1951

John got married to Sarah, who we all called Sally, in 1950 and moved away. Sally's parents owned the Mucky Duck when it was the Gulf View Inn (and Andy Rosse Lane was Palm Avenue). They got married at Chapel by the Sea, as did Pauline and I, and I was best man.

The Bailey boys took turns serving as best man. I did it for John, Sam did it for me, and John did it for Sam.

Sally's family was here in the summer of 1949 and she and my brother John didn't exactly get off to a great start. Sally's father, Roy Wedekind, thought he saw a boat on fire way out in the gulf. Now, there was no communication with the outside world on Captiva unless by shortwave radio. John got all bent out of shape because he said nobody had heard anything about a boat being on fire and that the old man was crazy. Mr. Wedekind wanted Daddy to notify the Coast Guard. John got all upset about that, I don't know why.

John described Sally to me in a very uncomplimentary manner. Pauline and Sally got to be friends, though. The three of us would play cards – canasta was all the rage then – before we got married. The following year there was a party at the Engles' house, and I asked John if he would invite Sally. I think he said a few expletives before he said "No."

I said, "At least will you be polite to her?" Finally, very begrudgingly, he agreed to that. She walked down from Gulf View Inn and they met in the yard. Something clicked right then and there. They were married less than a year later. He never forgave her father, though. He was obnoxious about it. It used to embarrass me the way he talked.

After John got married, he spent very little time on Sanibel. First he lived in Florida and worked for Swift & Co. in Ocala. Then he got a job in Arkansas where they had fancy cattle instead, but he was more interested in working with beef cattle.

So he came back to Florida and set up house in Bartow. His children were born there and they later moved to Jacksonville because the air was so polluted in Bartow with the phosphate mining. But John was worried about the pollution because it was bad for the cattle — not the children, the cattle. That always makes me kind of laugh and shake my head at the same time.

He was in Bartow roughly from1952 to 1961 and then went to Jacksonville and was there for the rest of his life. He was retired and visiting in Sanibel, it just so happened, when he went into Hope Hospice where he passed away. John died in 2000. Som said he died from "takin' too many pills."

It's not that John didn't care for Sanibel. He just cared for cows and horses and they weren't here. When we were growing up, we had mules but they were labor animals, and by the time we were grown up, even they weren't on the island anymore.

John and Sally

John's three children are Angela, who lives in Jacksonville; and twin boys Clark and Craig. Craig was killed when he was a sophomore in college. He was hit by a car crossing the street. I don't know whose fault it was. It doesn't make any difference, he's gone. Clark has taken over his father's business, the ranch. He comes down here with the mules for BaileyFest. Clark boards horses and people come and ride them. The horsey set, I call them; they're quite different sometimes. Then he had his own horses.

Sometimes we would go a long time without seeing John. It was a 350-mile trip over nothing but two-lane roads then. And we were all busy with businesses and children. He'd come down here occasionally; the cousins all know each other. Angela is the oldest, and then my daughter Anne is nine months younger.

Even though John was a sickly child, in college he was a cross-country runner, then a rodeo rider. Later on when he slowed down, he was a big calf roper. John just loved that kind of life.

One time when I was up at his house before Craig got killed, John had his two boys on horses. They were doing something with the cattle. He was barking out

John and his mules

I still miss my brother John.

orders to the dogs and the horses and the boys, and John was in hog heaven.

Meanwhile, about the time his sons were marrying, Daddy was enamored with a woman named Florence Hamlet. She decided to marry someone else, though, and gave Daddy the news via telegram. It was another heartache to him.

After Uncle Ernest died in 1954, things that had value to my brothers and me and to our wives – be it a cup, a piece of furniture, whatever – were laid out on the dining room table where we used to play ping pong when we were boys. We picked things out, then we traded. We went through it all – furniture, lamps, books. There were three big volumes of Shakespeare and we each took one. I would like to reunite those volumes and put them in the Sanibel Library. What was left over from that day, as far as I was concerned, was mine because I bought my brothers' interests in the house a few years after Uncle Ernest died.

Our little house was fine for a couple and their dogs, but we wanted children.

Our little house on the gulf was just fine for a young married couple starting out. It was just the two of us and our dogs, but Pauline and I wanted children. We tried everything under the sun that was available at the time to have a child but nothing worked. Finally we applied to several places to adopt. A doctor friend, Dr. Ernest Bourkard (we called him "Bokie") who came down to Sanibel to fish, was in my house and asked if we wanted a baby and I said we would only take a boy. I was adamant. I was really serious about it. Evidently, he could see beyond my foolishness, as you'll see. Soon after, we were over in Miami while I was on a buying trip and went to a party where we met a lady who was a very close friend of Aunt Char's. When we got back to our hotel about 1 a.m., there was a message in my box to call Bokie in Tampa. The first thing that crossed my mind was something happened to Sam. But Bokie said, "I have a baby girl, will you take her?" Even now I get choked up remembering. I said, "Of course we will." I couldn't talk any more than that; I had to hand the phone to Pauline. And that was our daughter Anne.

Three or four days later they hand me this little thing all wrapped up. I was afraid to touch a child. By the time we got home, I was changing diapers and everything. In those days, your thumb ended up looking like a pin cushion from changing diapers, not like today.

We adopted two more girls after that, but we still wanted a boy. The rule was, though, that you had to wait a year between adoptions. Because we had put in for adoption at a lot of different places, we were told we had a baby in Fort Myers with a Dr. Selden, who was

Pauline with our first daughter Anne

Pauline's doctor – that was Mary Mead. Shortly after – it was just a few days – the place in St. Petersburg told us that we had another baby, a boy. But when they heard we had just gotten a baby, they said we couldn't have two and would have to wait a year. Well I'll tell you, we waited one year and one second to adopt our boy Patrick.

Then Mother Nature surprised us and Pauline got pregnant; two years later Jane was born on the same birthday as Mary Mead, May 19.

I wasn't in the room for Jane's birth. I can't see the father being in the room for the birth. I can't see that. While I was downstairs waiting for it to happen, I donated some

blood. Now they won't take my blood anymore because I had to have a pig valve put in a few years ago. I say, "Take my blood, people need it." I've even tried to sneak it but everybody knows me and they tell me, "Get out of here!"

Pauline and I lived in our little beach house quite comfortably for a time. When the second baby came along and we had a dog to boot and the homestead was empty – Daddy died in 1952 and Uncle Ernest in 1954 – I knew we would have to either expand our house on the

Sam, Cookie, me, Sally, John and Pauline

Rebuilding the porch after Hurricane Donna, 1960

A party on the old porch

gulf or move to the homestead. I asked Pauline, not sure how she would feel about it, "Do you think we ought to live there?" and she agreed, or perhaps acquiesced. She could see I really wanted to go back to the homestead. I told my brothers I would like to have the homestead, and I purchased their interests. It was all right with them. Pauline did a lot of renovating and I was back home, now with a wife and growing family.

Sam's family was growing, too, and he really wanted a boy, same as I did. He already had two girls when his wife Cookie was pregnant with their third child. Sam had been a ladies' man. All the girls were attracted to him like a magnet, and a lot of mothers wanted Sam to be their son-in-law. He met Cookie and she and her family didn't care, and he never had anybody act like that before. And he was attracted to her.

The children loved to spend time on the ledge over the door into the kitchen as demonstrated here by my daughter Susan.

She was a school teacher in Sarasota – I think she taught physical education.

Cookie had a friend Hazel she wanted me to meet but each time I was going to be introduced to her she was never there, so I named her Harvey the Rabbit for the movie with Jimmy Stewart. I finally saw her the day Sam got married. I knew John's wife Sally better than I knew Cookie because Sally was here on the island and we played cards and things like that together. We only did things with Cookie occasionally.

Sam was traveling a lot in those days with his football team, and their third baby was real late coming. Sam would make a collect call not to his wife Cookie but to the unborn baby. He would ask for "Bo" Bailey — a boy's name. He'd say, "Is Bo Bailey there?" and

Cookie would answer, "No." This way, he knew the baby hadn't come and he didn't have to pay for a call. Sam's girls are named Tee, Toy and Tye, but I'm not sure how they came up with those names. Cookie's name is Thelma, and her maiden name is McCook. All her sisters at one time or another have also been called Cookie.

Cookie is always ready to go, up for anything. My brothers and I were sitting around Sam's house in Tampa after one of his ball games, and somebody somehow got to talking about go-go girls. I honestly didn't know what she was talking about so she said, "I'll show you." No one else wanted to go. So we went to this joint. The Black Hole of Calcutta would have looked like Las Vegas' main street compared to this joint, it was so dark. Here comes this guy up to the table, who turned out to be the sports editor of the Tampa Tribune. He recognized Cookie and wanted to know who she was with. So here's Coach Bailey's wife out in this joint with a strange man and he's got to be thinking, "Wow, have I got a story!" Then when he found out the man was Sam's brother, you could just see that man deflate, like you'd stuck a pin in a balloon – he'd lost his hot story. We had some good times.

Pauline outside the homestead with Jane, Mary Mead and Anne

Then my wife Pauline's illness started on a Saturday night while I was working. After we ate dinner I went back to the store and she called me on the phone and said she had an awful headache. I came home and she was on the floor beside the toilet vomiting, in terrible shape.

I took her to the hospital, and they took her in an ambulance to Tampa. Our doctor friend Bokie, who was instrumental in helping us adopt Anne and Susan, arranged to get Pauline admitted to the hospital. We went up there and they packed her in ice and one day she actually regained consciousness. She got considerably better, a marked improvement. The next day she was gone. It turned out to be a brain aneurysm. She had lived only a few days. I wasn't beside her bed when she died. I asked Bokie later, "You knew she wasn't going to live, didn't you?" He said, "Yes, but we did everything we could."

It was a hard thing that she died on Sam's birthday, January 29, 1965, because Sam really liked her. That's why I don't understand why he really didn't show much of a liking for our children. Sam's general attitude about my wife and the kids prevented me from being as close with him as I had been at one time, and he had no reason. The only thing I can think of is he practically adored Pauline – they went to school together, as I said – and he was visibly upset. When I got married the second time, to Adelaide, I might have done it a little too fast after Pauline's death; that could be the reason why he didn't accept Adelaide. But there was no reason for him not to accept my wife June. Of course, she's as bullheaded as he was – that may have something to do with it. I never asked him. But at least one of my children has said that Sam never said one word to her, ever. He had never been very warm with my children although he never went out of his way to be ugly to them. He just didn't give them the time of day. But we're all crazy, I suppose, in one way or another. The cousins were always great. Tee, Toy and Tye used to visit and we have pictures of everyone together as a family, including John's children, Angela, Clark and Craig.

My two sisters-in-law, Sally and Cookie, although I didn't see Cookie as often as I did Sally, stayed involved with my family and did a lot of things to help us out when I was alone with the children.

As a widower with five very young children, I needed help. Jane was less than a year old when her mother died. I interviewed people hoping to find help. One woman came down and lasted about four days. She just didn't fit in. She seemed dictatorial and not very loving. She reminded me of someone who would be in charge of an orphanage in Daddy's time.

I paid Esperanza Woodring to help, and I'm sure she did more than she got paid for. She was a tremendous help, as were Mary Gault, Fanetta Stahlin, Dottie McQuade and others. I had a lot of friends on the island. Still do.

Besides all the help these women gave me with the children, when I re-married I had not yet done anything with Pauline's things that were in the house that my new wife would soon call her own. These women took everything and put it all in the attic. It was a very nice and considerate thing to do, because the next woman doesn't like to see the first wife's things. That's a personal thing. I didn't see Pauline's things again until 2011 when we had to clean out the house to sell it to the Sanibel-Captiva Conservation Foundation.

DADDY'S DEATH

Not long after my brothers and I all married (me for the first time), Daddy passed away in 1952. Daddy was not much for doctors. Not long before he died, he went to Fort Myers for a checkup and in retrospect he was very jovial about it: "They couldn't even find a little old cancer," he said. I have a feeling right then and there they told him he had cancer but he wouldn't tell anyone. He didn't seem to have a lot of pain. When he got sicker, I drove him up to the hospital in Tampa.

When Daddy told you he didn't feel good, you paid attention because he was not a complainer. He was just sick; I don't think he had any pain, but maybe he was just a tough old buzzard and never mentioned it. To us, he didn't seem to have any pain. But even the doctor – yes, Bokie again – could see Daddy was dying, although Daddy couldn't see it.

John came in from Arkansas and we were staying in Sam's house. John and Sam had gone home to get some sleep and I sat first vigil. It wasn't very long; it was rather quick in fact. It was the first night we put Daddy in the hospital. Now, Daddy had a habit when he was upset with himself – he would wave his hand like he was waving you away or making

light of a situation and maybe say, "Oh, pshaw," which was something he said quite often or when he was disgusted with himself. I never heard him cuss. When he waved his hand in this manner, the nurse thought he was trying to pull out his oxygen. You couldn't talk to him at that point. I was sitting in the room reading when the nurse gave me the impression the situation wasn't very good for Daddy. She said to me, "Do you know how sick your father is?" She frightened me, the way she said it. I rushed out to phone my two brothers and when I got back to the room, he was gone. It was stomach cancer.

As I've said, Daddy wanted to be buried in Virginia, so we just took his body right up to Richmond and had no kind of memorial service on Sanibel. We were all in Tampa with Daddy. We realized right away we made a mistake. I don't like funerals, but people like to say goodbye.

ADELAIDE, RAISING THE CHILDREN

It was just one and a half years after Pauline's death that I married Adelaide (April 1966), whom Pauline had known. Adelaide seemed interested in me, and I was also concerned about the children having a mother. One time driving by Jerry's of all places, my daughter Anne asked me, "When are we going to have a real mother?" as opposed to the parade of kind people who had been helping to care for the children. That sort of got to me.

Me with my second wife Adelaide. We were married in 1966 and divorced in 1974.

Adelaide lived in Heron House on West Gulf Drive and had been married three times before our marriage. She had a son, Will Compton. After our divorce, she remarried her second husband and they subsequently divorced again.

Heron House had a studio called Mouse House where Adelaide would draw. She moved into the homestead and did some renovations, just as Pauline had done. I think the marriage was a little bit of a rebound thing for me and happened too fast. It lasted eight years, though, and Adelaide contributed some great things to our family. I don't know for sure where she was from. Her parents were living in Cape Cod but her father had some close connections with Florida. He worked for JC Penney for a long time and played in John Phillip Sousa's band.

We always spent a few weeks in the summer in Cape Cod. I would stay home and work, like Daddy used to do when I was a kid and our family went to North Carolina. Adelaide and I eventually bought a home up there, then divorced a little while after that. I didn't want her to leave, but once she did, I didn't want anything to do with her and I wouldn't let her back. I just wanted to pull the curtain down; it was probably some anger and pride on my part. She didn't want to go through with a divorce and make it final, I'm not sure why, but I insisted it wasn't healthy to live in a gray area. The kids went back and forth between us for a while. I think they wanted to live wherever they thought they could get away with the most, which invariably meant with Adelaide. In my daughter Jane's case, she didn't know any other mother but strangely enough she was the least attached to Adelaide of all my children. Mary Mead was probably the most attached to her; I don't know exactly why. But my children had already lost one mother and they didn't want to lose another.

Me reading to Anne and Susan

Being married of course was a help with the children and they got along with Adelaide — better than I did. I never said anything derogatory about her to the children, though. They were very young and basically for the three youngest, she was their mother. Unfortunately, it seemed I turned out to be just like one of Adelaide's previous three husbands. It happens.

During the eight years after our divorce, I was involved with many things around the island. After a while, I dated quite a bit; I suppose the ladies liked me. When I married June, who is Canadian, one of the local ladies told me she had a bone to pick with me and I thought, "Oh no, what have I done now?" And that woman said to me, "With all the local ladies here on the island, you had to import one?"

Anyway, I didn't have to have babysitters much during the time I was single, as the children were at school. Adelaide was a big advocate of private and boarding schools during and after our marriage. We went that route primarily because Adelaide was the wife and mother at the time and that was the way things were. Plus she had influence with the children.

Anne went to Cypress Lake High School in Fort Myers for her freshman and sophomore years and then took a trip with me to North

I married my wife June on April 10, 1982 and we have enjoyed a long and happy marriage.

Horsing around with Sam's daughter Tee and my daughters Anne and Susan

Carolina and Virginia looking at girls' schools. I liked one in North Carolina but they told her she would have to work hard so she didn't want to go there (she'll dispute that to this day) and in 1972 ended up going to a school in Richmond, Virginia called St. Catherine's. Her second cousin had gone to the same school years before. It was part day school and part boarding school. She also went to Outward Bound, which is a nonprofit educational organization and expedition school. It offers expeditions as a way for students to experience adventure and challenge. Anne liked it. Then she went to Jacksonville for college, then to an all-girls school in Massachusetts that had to do with retailing. She was also on a ship school sailing across the Atlantic from Woods Hole, Massachusetts, and that school was focused on the sailing rather than a regular school curriculum.

Susan didn't want to go to any school; she was a rebel. I don't remember why or what she was doing, but one time she was someplace she wasn't supposed to be over at Cypress Lake High School. There's a huge playground or courtyard between two buildings – or

Susan, Anne and Cousin Tee, 1960

there was at that time. One time I came in trying to find her and there were a bunch of people there. I tore into her in a loud voice. The girl who was with her took off like a scared rabbit. I don't remember what I did to punish Susan. She used to hide behind the house with a blanket during school hours to sleep. How I snuffed that out, I don't know. She went to a lot of schools – Canterbury School, and one in New York and later one in Texas. Before she was even 18, she crawled through the fence and just took off, disappeared. She was good at that. She's gotten some education since then and is in Tampa now. She really wants to help the underdog in life but always seems to go about it the difficult way. She adopted four kids, and they were raging hyenas. Two or three have really tamed down; she did a wonderful job with those kids, teaching them manners and a better attitude toward life.

Mary Mead, who most people call Mead except me, was closer to Adelaide then any of the other children. She also went to the ship school like Anne. It was called Flint School and was a regular school with a full curriculum that took place on a ship that sailed all over the world. Mary Mead started out in Bermuda, worked her way through the Caribbean, and across the ocean to Denmark and France and all sorts of places. She got some excellent experience and ended up graduating in Monaco. I actually was able to be there because, as luck would have it, our grocers co-op had a trip to Spain at the same time. In those days it was quite a bargain to make trips like that. Anne and Merrell Rushworth were

Bottom to top: Susan, Anne, Mary Mead and Patrick

traveling around Europe and they were able to make it to the graduation as well. Then she went to some technical schools in North Carolina where she started dating Richard Johnson. Now Mary Mead and Richard are married and own Bailey's General Store; she is manager of the produce section, and that department has blossomed under her leadership.

My son Patrick went to Canterbury School and then to a school in Tennessee for a short period. He was even at school overseas on the ship with Mary Mead for a period of time but that didn't work. He just drifted around Sanibel after that. Then he sort of went out on his own. It's caused a rift mostly between Patrick and me. Even so, I recognize he's a very intelligent person.

Jane was a wild and wooly one but in a different way. She was so bad at one point, she got kicked out of school. She was always being called on the carpet. The children took after their

My son, Patrick

Me with Mary Mead, Jane and Anne

father, I guess – they just couldn't behave. But Jane finally settled down and after she simply couldn't tolerate the school she was at, she went to live with Sally and John up in Jacksonville. After that she went to prep school in Mississippi. It was an Episcopal Church school right on the river. The school had two groups, Devils and Angels, and they always competed against each other – not just in sports, but in reading and other academic things. And she was an Angel – if ever there was a misnomer!

She graduated from there and went to Brevard and we took everything in the car but the kitchen sink – and I'm not sure she didn't put that in there when I wasn't looking. Then she went on to Clemson University and got a Florida teaching certificate. She came and worked in the store for a little while and met her husband Mike who now works for the U.S. Fish & Wildlife Service. He had been married before and had two children. They weren't married at the time and I wasn't wild about that set-up. He got transferred to near Gainesville.

Jane's daughter Annabelle with Tye's daughter Sanabelle

Now they're in Atlanta because he got a promotion to Okefenokee. She taught school before adopting her child, Annabelle, who is severely handicapped. I am so proud of Jane for adopting that child and taking such good care of her. It's just remarkable. When Annabelle came along from the Children's Home Society, Jane and Mike decided moving to Atlanta and taking care of this new baby was too much all at once, so Mike almost didn't take the job. I said, "You have to do it," so I helped them out.

Jane was less than nine months old when her mother Pauline died – she was still part-time nursing – so she probably has no conscious recollection of her mother at all. I don't believe she feels differently from the other children because she's not adopted, and I don't remember anybody throwing that up to her. They would have gotten a stern lecture from me if they had. It was like she didn't have a mother. She had an up-and-

Nothing matters more to me than my family.

down relationship with her stepmother: one week she would like Adelaide, the next week she wouldn't.

My children have all done great things in their lives. As teenagers of course, children know so much more than their parents. They think, "How dumb can they be?!" Then a few years later all of a sudden they think, "What did Daddy do? He's smart all of a sudden!"

After the divorce, the children initially went with Adelaide to Heron House for a while instead of staying with me, and then it was back and forth and off and on. Then the kids were more or less at school. Except for Anne, they all went to Canterbury School for a while, then left that school for various reasons, as I've explained. For two or three summers during the marriage, the family stayed at Heron House, and we also went to Adelaide's family's home in Harwich on Cape Cod, where they lived at that time.

After the divorce from Adelaide, I lived alone at the homestead for about eight years, roughly from 1974 to 1982. I didn't particularly like living alone, but the kids were in and out. Anne and Patrick had people coming and going. A friend of Anne's came to spend a night or two and then got a job as a cook at what is now the Blue Giraffe (it was Duncan's then). Anne went on her way and the girl, Sandy Jackson (now Motley), stayed for about a year. Later, John's daughter Angela came, too, and stayed for nine months.

JUNE

Then I met June in December 1980.

It was through my friend Keith Trowbridge that I met my current wife June. After a Kiwanis vs. Lions softball game – which my Lions lost – we went down to The Jacaranda (it was Scotty's then) to pay Al Duncan, the owner, the $15 we owed him for losing. (I still have my baseball uniform, by the way.)

Keith was about to marry June's sister, Doris. He was walking out when I was walking in, and he introduced me to June. When we met it must have struck some kind of a note – evidently she appealed to me in some way.

Keith Trowbridge, June, me, her sister Doris

We were at Scotty's at first, which was unusual for me, but I had to pay Duncan the money I owed him. Then we ended up staying at Keith's house until 5 a.m. Al Duncan (who was Keith's cousin, so we had an "in") fell asleep under the piano. That was in December 1980.

In January 1981, Keith and Doris went to Winnipeg, Canada, and I went with them to see June. She met

At the 2012 Cracker Fest on Sanibel June has helped me to travel more and I am very grateful for that.

me at the airport in a car with the back window broken out and it damn near froze me to death. I remember she put me in a hotel on the corner of Portage and Main. I came home after that visit and then Keith and Doris got married in June, so I went up to Canada again for the wedding.

For me to go back to that cold climate, you knew I was serious about June. Holy catfish, it was cold – and it wasn't January; it was June! That wind on

Above: June and I at Victoria Falls

Left: We are in Alaska

the corner – I get cold even now thinking about it. June took me out to play golf. It was fairly late in the afternoon and it started getting dark and was raining. You couldn't find the ball for all the leaves on the ground. We were walking, sopping wet. That night we were supposed to go to a reception at the hotel. We went to my hotel for me to get dressed and June went on to the reception. When I walked in, she said, "Where have you been?

Christina and Casey Shaw, Linda and Thomas Stevens, and Bruce Shaw - these are June's children and their spouses.

At that point, let's just say the fish hook was there but it wasn't set yet. We got married on April 10, 1982 at Keith Trowbridge's house on the bay with my son Patrick standing up for us as Best Man. June is the person in my life who helped me to travel more. I had been on my own for eight years before I married her, and now we've been married for more than 30 years. I used to think "30 years ago" was ancient history, and now 30 years goes by and –

143

poof, it's gone before you can turn around – a third of my life. June got me out playing golf and we've taken many golf trips. I play the ladies' tees, she plays the pro tees, gives me two strokes and a 35 handicap and she still beats me. We've been on many Lions' trips, trips to Canada, Australia and many other wonderful places. I owe that to her, and I'm grateful.

MOSQUITO CONTROL

There's no way to express how important it was to this area to get the mosquitoes under control. John Kontinos tells a frightening story that really expresses the need we faced to do something. He had a restaurant called Coconut Grove – it's now George & Wendy's Corner Grill – and he would walk across the field at six o'clock in the morning and go in and start up the restaurant. Mosquito Control would come around in the evening or late at night and fog. His area had been fogged the night before, but when he got up close to that light pink building and looked up, it looked black. He thought the fogger had accidentally sprayed black oil all over the building. But as he approached, that black mass just lifted off of the building and started chasing him. He had mosquitoes in his eyes, in his ears, his nose, his throat. He was being suffocated. He fumbled for his keys, frantic, and says it's the most frightening thing to ever happen to him.

The mosquitoes would cover your skin almost completely. If you held your arm out and shook a can of pepper all over it, it would look about the same. If you had to do something where you had to hold still for a while, you would just grit your teeth and do it.

The old-timers (me) will say you could swing a quart cup and get a gallon of mosquitoes. A bit of an exaggeration, but I would wake up and there'd be mosquitoes all over the screen, sometimes so that it impeded your sight and restricted the light that was coming in. That is not an exaggeration. You may think some of these stories about blocking out the sun and the black wall are tall tales, but let me tell you, they're absolutely true. I lived here and my family farmed here, and we just put up with those things. But dealing with those mosquitoes would sap your strength; it would tire you out.

I remember after the 1944 hurricane, we had a little telephone line on the island. There were three men – two others and myself – working on the line and one of them was about as tough as you can get, and I thought I was pretty tough, too. I was in the Army at the time and got a 30-day leave to help clean up the island. Well, we had to quit at three o'clock in the afternoon because of the mosquitoes. They were just so bad, it just sapped all your strength. I remember Miss Lettie Nutt's little house – it was wrecked in that hurricane. The mosquitoes got in there and you could go in the window tracks

Miss Lettie Nutt's house

where the mosquitoes had gotten caught and just pick up double handfuls of dead mosquitoes from the edge of the windows. In fact, there was just enough sand outside her door that with the piles of dead mosquitoes on top, the doorway was blocked. Light fixtures would fill up with them until finally someone would smell something – cooked bugs! The mules, when they'd work during the day, you'd look under their bellies and they would just be black with mosquitoes. You see, they could get the mosquitoes off their backs by throwing their tails but their solid bellies would exposed and vulnerable. As soon as you turned those mules loose in the lot, they'd head right for the ground and just roll and roll and roll to get rid of the mosquitoes. I'll bet that felt good.

So I'm not exaggerating. Do you know mosquitoes can kill a full-grown cow? We didn't have cows here, we couldn't. But on the mainland they could kill a full-grown cow because the cow would breathe them in and they would get in its lungs, eventually suffocating the cow.

Of course, I grew up with mosquitoes and most times when I'd go to sleep at night and wake up in the morning, my bed would be full of bloody spots all over where I'd killed mosquitoes in the night, either inadvertently by rolling over or by slapping them.

We used Bee Brand Insect Powder in those early days. It was pyrethrum in powder form and you'd burn it and the smoke would actually not only drive the mosquitoes away but kill them. We had swishers at the front door to brush off as many mosquitoes as possible before coming into the house.

The mosquito problem gave Sanibel a bad reputation, as you can imagine.

The state was always trying to do something about the mosquitoes. As far as the Mosquito Control District goes, most everything we accomplished in those early days came out of the Sanibel Community Association: the Fire Department, the Audubon Society, and it was the same with Mosquito Control. The state of Florida had districts, and we got some money from the state to help us out. Wayne Miller worked for the state, and he came over and helped Sanibel and Captiva do certain things. There were "x" dollars for Lee County, Collier, Boca Grande, Fort Myers, Fort Myers Beach, Sanibel, and Captiva – all had Mosquito Control Districts. There were four separate districts, the first in Lee County established in 1949 at Fort Myers Beach. In 1950, Fort Myers set up a program, and in 1953 Sanibel-Captiva and Boca Grande established districts. So there were four separate programs, four boards of commissioners, four tax levies, and all four districts together comprised less than eight percent of the county. Naturally somebody started making noise about forming one overall district, and the state said, "Consolidate and spend your money more efficiently."

We worked through the Fort Myers Chamber of Commerce. I was on the board and on the committee, and we got consolidation through and formed the county-wide entity in 1956, but Alva and Fort Myers Beach decided to stay separate – and they are still independent districts. All were autonomous taxing authorities that could levy taxes and hire people.

The original commissioners for Sanibel and Captiva on the Mosquito Control Board were Johnny Wakefield, Dick Kearns, and me. Later there was Wayne Miller running it, and John Kontinos took my place when I became a Sanibel city councilman.

When the districts were consolidated, the new board took one commissioner from each previously existing board. The way I was appointed was I was late to the meeting, so I was it. I couldn't convince them differently. I eventually had to get off the board to run for city council on Sanibel. But I was on the Sanibel-Captiva Mosquito Control Board from the time it was created in 1953 until the consolidated board was created in January 1958 – about five years. Then I was elected to the consolidated board on November 12, 1957. All told, I served for 26 years if you include all of Sanibel's prior efforts that started in 1949.

I suppose I helped found the Sanibel district, not so much Lee County Mosquito Control. Something had to be done. The tourist season on Sanibel was very restricted, maybe 10 or 12 weeks long. The rest of the year, most people just didn't consider the island habitable.

We didn't formulate any methodology or anything on Mosquito Control – we hired entomologists. We were working with the state and Wayne Miller, trying to implement mosquito control . We had people here testing the water and doing wells and publicizing.

I enjoyed it; I enjoyed most everything I did. I don't say it was the highlight of my life. It was an interesting experience and I learned a lot, particularly from Wayne.

For example, Sanibel is probably the world's largest producer of salt marsh mosquitoes. You measure mosquito populations with what they call the New Jersey Light Trap. This is a device with a light in it that attracts mosquitoes. There's a fan that sucks them

A New Jersey light trap, used to measure the mosquito population. On Sept. 15, 1950 Sanibel broke every known record in the world.

inside and a jar of toxin that kills them. You run the lights from dark until daylight. Then you count the collection and that tells you the extent of the problem. Generally, 25 mosquitoes in a trap constitute an annoyance; if you have fewer than 25, you probably wouldn't know there were any around. One hundred mosquitoes are a problem. With 100, Mosquito Control's phone starts ringing off the hook. If you get up to 2,000 in a night, they get in your throat, in your ears, and they boil around your legs in direct sunlight. Mosquitoes are very much of a problem at 2,000.

It's a fact that on September 15, 1950, on Sanibel – and not in the back woods, but right at the ferry landing – in one trap, in one night, we collected 365,000 salt marsh mosquitoes, of which 98,000 were males and 267,000 were females, the ones that bite. As far as we know, that's the largest light trap collection that's ever been taken anywhere in the world. And we believe the collection was even larger than that final figure, because the mosquitoes filled up the trap, and a five-gallon lard can under the trap, and clogged the fan that was drawing them inside. Because it overflowed, we wouldn't really know how many were in there but it was by far a world's record.

To be clear in my explanation, you don't really count each mosquito – you count a sample and weigh them and determine the count that way. I don't know what it was about that area around the ferry landing but for some reason that seemed to be one of the worst spots. You could always find mosquitoes there when you couldn't find them anywhere else.

In the late 1940s there were flight range studies done here. Mosquitoes were hatched under radioactive conditions, then the adults were allowed to just fly and were chased down with Geiger counters. A number of the mosquitoes that were released on Sanibel were picked up in LaBelle. So the flight range is such that mosquitoes that start out in the coastal areas can affect everybody in the county. We used that as a justification to spend more money on Sanibel to control the mosquitoes.

The two types of mosquitoes we battle, in plain language, are:

- Little gray ones that bite. They lay their eggs on dry land near water. Whenever the water rises and covers them, they hatch – but not all at the same time. They can fly 25 to 30 miles.

- Rain barrel mosquitoes. They breed around homes in any standing water – a tin can, an old tire, a birdbath. Sometimes there are a lot of these mosquitoes up north.

If it rains a lot, people think we're going to have a lot of mosquitoes but it's actually just the opposite. Because these mosquitoes lay their eggs on dry ground – that is, where there's no standing water – it's usually moist but it will soon flood. A lot of us are used to northern climes where you have so-called "rain barrel" mosquitoes that breed in standing water, but that is minimal around here. It's the salt marsh mosquitoes that cause the problem. If the weather is wet and dry, wet and dry, they hatch out.

The idea of controlling mosquitoes in the larval stage is two-fold: mosquitoes bite you, and they lay eggs. If you get them in the larval stage, you escape all of that.

A high school called the district one time and told us, "The mosquitoes are killing us." Well, nobody else had any mosquitoes at that time. We sent someone over and it turned out to be a problem in just one classroom. It turned out the mosquitoes were hatching out of aquariums they had there. And the teacher in that room was a science teacher! I thought that was the funniest thing. If it had been an English teacher it wouldn't have been as bad, but a science teacher!

Others would call the district and complain, "You folks haven't been out here spraying lately." We'd ask them, "Do you have any mosquitoes?" and they'd say, "No, but the truck hasn't been here." Some people expected you to come by like garbage pickup, every Tuesday, whether they needed it or not.

We had one funny thing happen when we first started out with the fogger. We had two different kinds of little portable foggers we put on the back of a truck. One of them was a Dyna Fog, which was really like a jet engine. It made one heck of a racket. What we used to do was to go around people's homes early in the morning and sometimes late at night, depending on the circumstances, and fog so people could have relief. Well, this one

> ... she runs out of her room, clear out of her bedroom, out into the yard in her nightgown.

woman's home was two houses down from the Island Inn. She was a very sedate lady, Mrs. McMillan. The road by her house went right by her bedroom window. Now this guy comes in there at about four or five o'clock in the morning with this Dyna Fog and she runs out of her room, clear out of her bedroom, out into the yard in her nightgown. She thought she was being invaded. Wayne says there are still people who'll pull off the road into a ditch when they see an airplane coming with smoke spewing out of both engines.

Wayne tells one story I love. A number of years ago the then new owner of Snug Harbor, the marina between Punta Rassa and town, called and asked Mosquito Control to keep its planes away from there, afraid it might kill the bait shrimp. I guess it could have killed them, so we started avoiding that area. Punta Rassa was just a little settlement by itself then, so it was easy to pass it by. About a month later, the owner called Wayne and

The Sanibel River is the lighter area running across the middle of this aerial photo.

asked if he could send airplanes down. He said he hadn't understood how bad it could get. Customers were getting out of their cars, walking about 30 feet, then turning around to get back in the car to leave. No customers, no bait sales.

We didn't just use foggers; there were other methods being developed. Some people believe the Sanibel River was actually created by the Mosquito Control program, but I have to rebut that. None of us ever called it the Sanibel River, first of all – we called it the bayou or the slough, because that's what it was. But it was deep enough that when the water built it up, it would flow like a river. The waters on Sanibel in the old days would be built up by rain, although not every year. The slough would build up and build up and build up until we called it a bayou. It would build up such a head of water that it would break through to the gulf (there's an overhead picture of this). One of the main places it broke through was down where The Colony is today. I've seen water going through there 50 or 60 feet wide, maybe sometimes 100 feet wide, three or four feet deep, and it would run out of there just like a river. Sometimes it continued for weeks at a time, or even two or three months. But it was nothing but fresh water with a built-up head. A storm would come in and fill the beach up, and the river would back up and maybe it wouldn't go back out again that year. Some years water stayed in it year-round and some years it didn't. And there was muck in that place. It would dry up and it would form big cracks, and you would think it was dry. When I was a little boy, I jumped off one of the bridges one time and of course I got my pants and my stockings and everything dirty and I had to go home and face my mother.

We never callled the Sanibel River anything other than "the slough" or sometimes "the bayou."

What Mosquito Control did with this bayou or slough was to deepen it and get a lot of that muck out of there so the water was there year-round. The concern of Mosquito Control was that in the winter, except for a few deep holes where there were alligators, it dried up and created a perfect mosquito-producing area. Part of the problem with maintaining a high enough water level to fight the mosquitoes was that the island actually leaks. It's like a sieve – it's sand and shell and the tide actually rises and falls in the middle of the island.

Wildlife Drive in the "Ding" Darling National Wildlife Refuge was constructed by Mosquito Control, so these efforts changed part of the landscape of Sanibel. Wildlife Drive was an effort to build a dike to control the water via artesian wells we could keep flooded. The wells were never built and the dike became Wildlife Drive.

Lee County still has the same potential for producing mosquitoes that it did when we set that light trap in 1950, and it will continue to have that potential.

Wildlife Drive in J.N. "Ding" Darling Wildlife Refuge was constructed by Mosquito Control.

HURRICANE DONNA

Donna was the hurricane that finally caught me on Sanibel after I had, by chance, missed so many.

We heard in advance this hurricane was coming and we made preparations for it. The warnings were different in 1960 than they are now. There wasn't as much TV and that sort of thing. We had a Mosquito Control Board meeting on Tuesday and it was forecast that Donna was coming up through the straits and headed our way, so we started getting set up and everything.

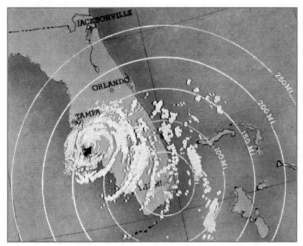

Hurricane Donna in 1960 was the first one to catch me at home on the island.

The island had started to grow by that time; we thought we had a lot of people then. We had a number of relatively young people, and I forget why or how, but for some reason we had formed a committee ahead of time to fight the hurricane. After it got here we did even more, so we were fairly well prepared. That was the first year the Mosquito Control District had two-way radios, and we got one of those radios because it was part of civil defense anyway. Dave Wooster was at our house and he had some kind of radio thing. His wife was in Fort Myers and she got on there and almost melted the radio, she was so angry – she really let him have it for being on Sanibel during a hurricane!

One of the first things I did was see that my aunt and her very close friend Christine Jenkins got the heck off the island way ahead of time. They were both scared and there was no reason for either of them to stay here and nothing they could do. I got them out of here someplace, I don't remember where – to a motel or to a friend of theirs.

Somehow, we just knew Donna was going to hit Sanibel. I don't know how you can feel it, but somehow you just feel it coming. Thursday I had a Mosquito Control Board meeting in Fort Myers and I came back on Friday and got ready for the hurricane to come.

Friday night, Donna was down in the Keys, going through the Straits down there, and it was going west then. Joe and Mary Gault battened down their house and came to the homestead with us. We stayed up until a fairly late hour and they went to bed, then we went to bed. Pauline had a radio on that kept blabbing on about the hurricane – Donna's doing this and Donna's doing that – and it was waking me up. Finally I said, "Turn that damn thing off! All it's doing is irritating me. The thing's coming and there's not a thing you can do about it and we need some sleep." She turned it off.

It was 30 minutes or an hour later that the fire siren went off. Being a volunteer fireman, I went three feet in the air, then charged up the road to see what was going on. There was a military helicopter coming in to evacuate the island. We were so mad we could spit wooden nickels, but we were supposed to go around and tell everybody to give them a chance to evacuate. It took me a while but I finally calmed down enough to do it. We went out telling people, and about half the people we told probably told us to go you-know-where.

But the military did take a lot of people off the island; by that time it was five or six o'clock in the morning and they had to stop. We had the Community House set up for a shelter but everybody left there. Nobody wanted to stay in the Community House. They started coming to our house in the morning. The only people who were here during the night were Joe and Mary Gault, and he was telling people who started calling, "Sure, come on down." Some of the people we didn't know too well and some we did. Colin Moore came over and Dave Wooster, and the Stahlins and Kearns and McQuades and some people who brought their two dogs. We put the dogs up in the attic. When the roof started leaking, everybody said the dogs were urinating. It leaked down around the chimney, not quite coming through. We ended up with 37 people in the house.

Donna came from the south with no land to disrupt it. The water came almost like a tidal wave. At the homestead, salt water came up from the back yard.

When I went down to the store, which was still on the bay in 1960, to check things and lock it back up, I brought home a whole bunch of hamburger meat. We had a gas stove and a gas refrigerator, so we were in like Flynn. Most of the hurricane was in the middle of the day. Finally the electricity went out and we had a little tiny auxiliary generator on the back porch. We didn't get much juice out of it, though. We had a radio set up inside and a truck outside. Of course we had a barometer sitting on the wall in the dining room and it kept going down, down, down.

The crowd I was with was not exactly a teetotaling group and everybody brought some kind of booze – a lot of booze. All of us in the group were the young people on the island and there wasn't anyone that didn't do a lot of drinking on Saturday night, but there wasn't one drink taken in that house that day. The wind started really howling about 10 o'clock in the morning – and even then not one drop of liquor was touched, not a drop. You've heard of hurricane parties? Not here. The coconut trees turned completely wrong side out. They're somewhat flexible, but it's rather frightening to see them like that. The side of the garage looked like it was flapping like a flag in the wind. You could feel the fear in the house. Pauline wouldn't let anyone go out – some of the kids wanted to – and we wanted to look at the buildings and see what more could be done to protect them if necessary. But she made everybody stay in the house. Damn right I was scared, and I'd be scared again.

I looked outside during the eye of Donna. The eye didn't pass over exactly and we didn't experience any dead center. The wind from Donna was coming in from the shore and the wind from some of the other hurricanes came in from the land. Donna came up through the Yucatan Channel, past Cuba, and came straight up the east coast and slammed into us. By contrast, the 1926 hurricane came across the state. In 1926, the salt water came up but it didn't get in our yard coming in from the bay side. With Donna, the water came up to the edge of our yard although it wasn't very deep. After the hurricanes of 1921, 1944 and 1945, water was all over the island. We could feel a shift in the wind, but the eye passed over inland of Sanibel. It was pretty close but not right here. If it had passed west of us, we'd have had a different story. The northeast quarter is usually the most intense quarter of a hurricane, and we didn't get that. But it was bad enough.

Along about two or three o'clock in the afternoon the storm began subsiding. However, the wind stayed strong and we didn't go out until much later. I was 39 years old but I was curious and nothing fazed me at all, and some of the rest of the group was the same way. We had no desire particularly to go out, but about nine o'clock we were out. It was complete devastation.

I'm walking down the road from the dock to the store.

Stahlin and a bunch went one way, and Wooster and I went the other because I was interested in going down to the store and the gas station. About 10 or 11 o'clock that night I started walking down the road to the store and got about halfway down Bailey Road and saw a piece of dock, one solid piece, and I said to myself, "Uh-oh, no store. That's the end of it." The road was just filled with branches. None of the big trees had fallen over but the limbs had broken. You had to crawl over those things, so I don't know how long it took us. I think it took us hours. But when I got down there, one corner of part of a warehouse that wasn't very well built was damaged by a tree, and a corner of a window was broken – it was a little window, up high. Part of my desk was wet, but we didn't lose a thing, not a sheet of paper. A little water had come in. I said facetiously at the time, "There's a mess on my desk!" I could feel the wind and rain on my face even as wet as I was. My desk was a mess and I kind of hoped – but not really – that Donna had destroyed all of the mess that was usually on my desk, but I didn't lose one paper. The storm had washed up that dock but not a drop of water was inside the building. Daddy built that building very solid and that land had been filled. We went around and entered on the back side, where the door was then. Of course there were no lights. I had a flashlight and I looked all around. I couldn't find any broken glass or broken windows yet I could feel wind. In the back part of the office I found the broken window pane. It had broken out completely, there was not a smidgen of glass – that's why you couldn't tell at first look.

A tremendous pine limb had fallen right between two buildings and just nicked one corner of both buildings, and that's all. If it had fallen six feet either way it would have crushed one or the other of the buildings, but it went right down in between them. It was just unbelievable luck.

It turned out we were very happy that we didn't stay in the Gault house because that same dock ended up in their living room. We were really lucky.

As for the house, part of the roof and porch were damaged, and one end of the house had shifted. I mean, it shook! We could see the garage and one side of the wall going back and forth in the wind. Rain came in through the double-hung windows, but it was just blowing in.

We went back to the house, where there were still a lot of people. Pauline put mattresses down; I don't even know where she got them. We put them on the floor and slept. When I woke up the next morning, most of the people were gone. And that's when we started to really clean up – and that's also when things started to rot. It was terribly hot ... oh, it was hot! And muggy. You're out there working in that sun with a saw and no water. We had a generator we got from Mosquito Control that we hooked up down at the store because we were the only source of food on the island. And after two or three days we started getting dry ice that came over on the ferry. They'd wheel it in and lower it on board. They were 100-pound blocks of ice that were only about 75 pounds probably by the time they got to the consumer because they would melt. We'd

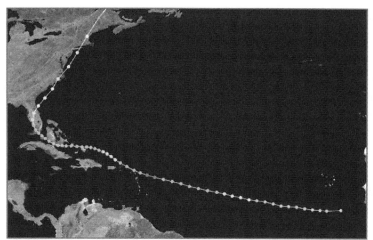

The track of Hurricane Donna across the Atlantic, turning on Florida and heading up the U.S. east coast

put gasoline in the generator every six hours; I think that's all it would run. It wasn't big enough to handle everything at the same time and the gas only lasted a certain amount of time. So I would get up at night and change the wires around so the generator would take care of a different part of the things that were being refrigerated. It's amazing how well it worked.

I would just come in and flop on the bed and sleep a few hours, set the alarm and get up. After about six days we were able to set up a shower so we could all shower. It sure felt good. We just kept going. We went around checking on everybody, too. Anywhere we knew there were people, we checked to make sure everybody was all right.

A hurricane is nothing to laugh at. Donna had sustained winds of 115 miles per hour and was a Category 4 when she passed through Sanibel. People who don't have business here should evacuate. Curiosity seekers, people who stay right on the water, I have no sympathy for them. But I also see no sense in leaving and going to the mainland and sitting in a building with big high glass windows without lights, water, beds, food, or friends. We all got together in groups and were better off than if we would have been here by ourselves. Of course it was a mess in one sense, but it was so much better. It's the water that's more dangerous than the wind.

Tom Billheimer left at one point with his two little kids Mike and Kim to escape the hurricane and I don't remember the exact sequence of events, but he went from place to place to place. Everywhere he went to spend the night, the hurricane hit there that same night and he was in a motel room with no water, no lights, and no way to get any food in a strange town.

If I were going to leave to get away from a hurricane, I'd go to Nebraska. No, I'm serious – go someplace the hurricane definitely won't be. Don't go to the East Coast or Louisiana or Gainesville. No, I'd get out. Most of us who stayed on the island through Donna did so because it was our home. There were people who lived on the gulf – the Jacks, Kearns, Stahlins, and McQuades, to name a few – who came inland. So as soon as it was over, they went to take care of their buildings. People will take care of their life investments. My home was in a building that, as far as I'm concerned, was as safe as almost any building can be, and we were able to help each other out.

We did have some problems with looting after the storm. We had Ralph Woodring and several people out in boats with guns because of it. I don't remember the exact details, but we had a patrol out. Lucky for the looters that none of them ran into Ralph. I was in charge of food because I was the grocer, so I remember more about that. It didn't amount to a whole lot. We got some dry ice and tried to dole it out, and we had other kinds of ice and some milk and stuff and managed to keep enough so that everybody had some.

I don't mean we gave them anything. There were a few people who came by looking for handouts. If they didn't really need a handout, though, they didn't get it. It made some people on the committee madder than it made me. People would come down to the store wondering where their handout was. And they sat on their big fat butts while their wives were out on the beach shelling. We just told them where to go. There just wasn't enough food to make food available to them, for one thing. I couldn't. And this wasn't supposed to be a handout. The rest of us were working hard, trying to get things opened up, and they weren't doing anything.

CHAPTER 5
OUR CITY

SANIBEL TRIES – AND FAILS – TO CONTROL ITS OWN DESTINY

In 1960 we put together a Planning and Zoning District – another effort that came out of The Community Association – which only lasted a few years, if that, before it eventually was overturned in court.

Lee County wanted 90,000 people on Sanibel, in high-rises (how else could you accommodate that number?). We said "enough is enough" so we wanted to put together our own land development code. I was on a committee of Sanibel people, and we met with the county commission.

Fort Myers Beach skyline

Marco Island skyline

**Two views of the Sanibel Island skyline,
the result of incorporation by the city and the regulations that followed.**

Because of Lee County's plans, Sanibel petitioned the legislature to be a separate taxing district able to tax up to 10 mils. We hired a couple of people to come down and lay it out for us, including a guy from Auburndale, Florida. The Central Board Review included Leroy Friday, Jimmy Jack, and others. Then the county commissioners got the legislators to declare the district null and void, and that was a big stimulus for Sanibel wanting to become a city.

Sanibel Tomorrow was formed, primarily by some winter residents who were as interested in the island as we were. Some of them had been involved islanders 20 years longer than almost anybody else.

They hired a big firm, planners from Philadelphia and attorneys from Chicago. We had legal experts as well. Fred Bostleman was the primary lawyer. They're the ones who actually wrote the stuff. Of course the thing's been so mutilated since then and transcribed into something a bureaucrat would write once they got a hold of it. In a way it's good because they consider only the sections that apply. If you want to put a chicken coop in your backyard, there are regulations that apply as to whether you can or can't.

I would have done things a little differently if I could have when the city was formed. If you ask anyone who was involved, they would probably say the same thing. It was a cooperative effort. In the same vein, if you wrote something, and another person wrote about the same thing, the versions would be different even though we would both be saying the same thing.

Politics! Here's how I feel about some elections in our country today, as I thought about it during the November 2010 election: I'm in a 22-story building and there's a raging fire on the 21st floor. There's no way an airplane can reach me so I have two choices: Jump or burn. I think I'd jump, You feel those flames licking at your feet; well, you have at least a tiny chance of surviving if you jump.

Any way you look at it, elections are a lot different now. In the early 1950s, somewhere along in there, we reached 100 registered voters on Sanibel and we thought, Whoopee! and that maybe now we would be heard in Fort Myers. That number is just registered voters and doesn't include children or black folks or winter folks. Today Sanibel's population is about 6,000.

Those 100 voters would cast their ballots in the fire house, which was located where the antiques store is now on Periwinkle Way next to Roadside City Park. When I started voting, we were voting in the packing house at the store. Uncle Ernest was the clerk in charge, then there were poll workers, and somebody was appointed to act as a sheriff (not associated with the sheriff's office) during the time the polls were open. We didn't really have a need for that, but that was the process we had to follow. I suppose some other places may have needed it; the practice goes back many years. Sam or John was the "sheriff" sometimes. They reveled in that.

When I moved the packing house up to the store, we decided it was too complicated to continue voting there, plus it was off the beaten path. Voting was moved to the fire house instead. We used paper ballots but it didn't take too long. The polls closed at 7 p.m. and we counted ballots and checked them with each other. The next morning we had to take the box to the Supervisor of Registration.

On Captiva, Charlie Knapp, then owner of the Casa Ybel hotel, was in charge. If somebody didn't vote he would take the ballot box to their house and have them vote. He would take the ballot box to Fort Myers on the ferry and was always the first to get recorded.

We also went to people's houses who couldn't get to the ballot box and took it around so they could vote. Maybe we shouldn't have done it, but it was on the up and up – it was still a secret ballot. Everything's changed today, of course. Everything.

THE CAUSEWAY

I was against building the causeway. Oh, was I. Oh, the causeway! To this day, I would just as soon they blow up that bridge. In fact, if anyone ever did blow up the bridge, I think the FBI would be knocking on my door asking, "Where were you?" (You know, before the causeway, if someone said "bridge," everyone knew that meant the bridge over to Captiva.)

Recently I was standing down at the bay where the old store used to be and someone wanted to take my picture. I realized the causeway was in the background and told them to take the picture facing the other way so you couldn't see the damn causeway at all.

This time I got caught in a picture with the causeway which I always try to avoid.

We had been talking about moving the store to the corner of Periwinkle Way and Tarpon Bay Road because the post office had moved away and the water transportation was dying down. You could see the change coming. Then the bridge was built and opened May 23, 1963, and I knew it was time to move the store.

Serious talk about the bridge had been going on for quite a number of years. The ferry company was going out and spending hundreds of thousands of dollars for boats and docks, and then there was a causeway and no use for them. It costs a lot of money to get a boat and knowing that the bridge was coming, there was no point in the ferry people spending that money for a boat with no chance to amortize their purchase. With bigger ferries, Sanibel could have done without the causeway. I have been on ferries that hold 20 to 30 cars.

It was Hugo Lindgren back in the 1950s who first wanted to bring mass development to Sanibel. He paid for engineering and feasibility studies, then went to the Lee County Commission and proposed the causeway. Lee County loved the causeway idea, but they loved the idea of development more and proposed the island could be built up to 90,000 units. Lindgren owned land here and naturally wanted to develop it. He is not one of my favorite people because of what he did, bringing the causeway to the island. What I would like to see is the "UN-abridged" Sanibel.

The causeway signaled the beginning of the end of Old Sanibel.

They wanted to build that first causeway to land at Bailey Road and I said no. I owned the land immediately contiguous to it on the west. I don't think I put "Hell, no" in my letter to the county, but I wanted to. I suppose they could have taken it by eminent domain but they chose not to. I hoped it would stop it but it just slowed things up a little bit, and I suppose that's all it did. I couldn't stop it no matter how much I didn't want to lose my island sanctuary. This was my home!

The store was closed in the afternoon the day the causeway opened, and the bridge was free that first day. I sat on the porch of my house and saw a solid stream of cars going by. To have that many cars on the island, I thought to myself, "Wait a minute – there's something wrong here!" It wasn't that long ago that there were probably only 100 cars on the whole island, and most of them were clunkers; there just weren't that many people here. As I sat there I thought, "I'm glad I'm not on that road."

Of course, now it's like that all the time. That night that the bridge opened, Pauline and I were invited to a party in Fort Myers at somebody's house. There was no striping on the causeway yet to mark the lanes. It was so strange to me to leave Punta Rassa and seven or eight minutes later be on Sanibel, with no waiting for the ferry. I don't know how to explain it, but that was a very eerie feeling, not to have to stop, get on the ferry, and so forth. What used to take 25 minutes took 10 minutes or less – it seemed like I was on Sanibel all of a sudden: "Wait a minute, I was just in Punta Rassa – what am I doing here on Sanibel?"

The store was really on a dead-end once the bridge opened. The only reason to go down Bailey Road was to go fishing or come to our store. People don't like coming down dead-end roads, even beautiful dead-end roads. There was a lot more beach back then, and Daddy had planted coconut trees. Today there's a plaque where the store used to be but it has the wrong date on it: it says it was there until 1964 instead of 1966. I've always been a stickler for facts, accuracy and grammar.

We were trying to figure out how to move the store, and where to move the store. We didn't own what is now Bailey's Center – it was owned by John Kontinos – but that's the location we wanted, and we moved the store in April 1966, renting from Kontinos. We expanded two or three times since then; I forget exactly the dates. We built an additional 50 feet to the west, looped around L-shaped in the back. Kontinos had built more shops in the center over the years we were renting from him. When we first got there, the center consisted of our store, the laundromat on the north side, and the beauty shop, and it ended right there. The laundromat had no water until the Island Water Association opened in Sanibel in November 1966. We had all fancy laundry machines and it was all built and ready but couldn't open. The surface water was too abrasive to use in the machines. Tourists would come around with a bunch of dirty diapers and just cringe to find there was no water yet. They would almost have tears in their eyes. That's when we finished building Bailey's Center. Island Water Association was in the works but still the water wasn't ready.

Later Kontinos built the rest of the center in two or three stages to get to the size it is today. Then we decided Bailey's needed space to enlarge the grocery store. We had our clothing store around 1974 that carried everything but formal clothing. We kept it until the early '90s, and my daughter Anne ran it at the end.

In 1981 we decided to really expand so we had this big plan where we were going to have a store that was going to be an arcade with shops in it and

behind it we would build a big store with a garden center run by Mike McQuade. When we went to the bank to borrow money, it was 22 or 23 percent interest. I kid you not. That ended that idea right quick. We pulled our horns way in and changed our whole plan. It's probably just as well, I don't know. In 1982, we built offices and a new space for The Grog Shop instead.

At the time, we knew we were going to buy the center from Kontinos. He had used up all his depreciation and was trying to get out, but we didn't have enough equity to borrow against, so he built the thing and then when he got it built, we bought it. I still don't own it – the bank owns it. But that's a cost of doing business. The shopping center is still under my ownership, but the store ownership has already been transferred to my son-in-law Richard Johnson and daughter Mary Mead. I don't notice much change though; things are still operating pretty much the way they always have. That's the way Richard wants it.

The new high span causeway with the old drawbridge still beneath it

The causeway's changed things, of course – some good, some bad. That's true of almost anything. When the proposal for this new higher causeway without a drawbridge came in 2003 to replace the original bridge, I had just exactly the opposite opinion of when the first

I felt if we were going to have a new bridge we should have the best bridge possible.

causeway was built. I felt if we're going to have a bridge, let's have the best bridge we can get. The thing that really got under my skin was when people were arguing over the new bridge and some said a high-span bridge would "ruin the view." The view was ruined when they built the damn thing in the first place in 1963.

I'm not big on change but I realize I have to do it, and I do it. Still, to this day I believe Sanibel could have survived quite well without the causeway. We wouldn't have as many tourists, that's true, and people wouldn't have built as much. It would be a different lifestyle, but that's what people who were against the causeway wanted. Life would be slower, growth would be slower. It could have worked if we increased the ferry service. Business would have demanded it. But when a ferry owner sees the handwriting on the wall that a bridge is coming, why bother?

Even the ferry, although I guess you could call it inconvenient, was kind of a family thing. If you would go to some show or play or party in Fort Myers, you would hire somebody or ask a friend with a small boat to take you to the ferry landing. You left

your car and that signaled the ferry captain to bring the car back to the island. We'd put the car on the ferry and he'd drive it over on the other side and we'd go over and drive it out. Sometimes it would be a few days before we paid them. Everybody on the island did that type of thing. They knew we would pay them. It was just a family-friendly thing. Nobody ever took the keys out of their car.

SANIBEL BECOMES A CITY

Early on I wasn't a big advocate of incorporation for Sanibel, but we soon found out we couldn't work with the Lee County commissioners.

The reasons I didn't feel too gung ho about Sanibel becoming a city were that taxes would go up, we would be responsible for the roads and so many other things. What I was hoping for desperately was to have better cooperation with the Lee County commissioners. But things were bad in Lee County government at that time — a couple of commissioners went to jail, a couple were connected with prostitutes. For years there wasn't a county commissioner who was re-elected except for one and that was only because he had a black man running against him. I'm sorry to say it, but that's the way things were then and it's true.

A number of groups formed when islanders started getting itchy to have more control over their own destiny. Sanibel Tomorrow was the big one, which I think was founded by Zee Butler, who went on to be a member of the first city council. Sanibel Tomorrow was working for the preservation and the implementation of home rule, making Sanibel a city. We needed to take care of our own destiny and it turned out to be the only way we could.

Even if we could have reached an agreement with the county, it might not have lasted. An ordinance or some other kind of agreement with the county wouldn't have given us a guarantee. The county commissioners change. You can pass an ordinance which becomes a law and a subsequent council can always pass another one

> **If that had worked and not been overturned, we might not have needed to form a city...**

that overturns it. Our attorney told me once that what you pass is the law of the land until some judge tells you it isn't. Of course if you pass something ridiculous barring all left-handed women from coming to the island, it would take a judge about five minutes to overturn it.

We thought we were doing great with Sanibel Tomorrow, and we got the density down as low as we could – to 18 units per acre; at least it was better than 30 or 40 units. That would have turned Sanibel into just a bunch of concrete and somewhere you might be able to see the water – occasionally. (Today, as a city, our permitted density is five units per acre for a little strip along the gulf, and everywhere else it's 2.2 per acre or less – much less than the county's vision.)

But we started out green as grass.

When we had taxing authority – Sanibel was a taxing district before it was a city, as I've said – and we wrote an ordinance zoning the island that was much better than the county's plan, as far as density, height of buildings, and much more. If that had worked and not been overturned, we might not have needed to form a city, but that is a big "if." The county commissioners were dead against our land code, and the legislature ultimately invalidated it. A taxing district was a common thing to some but the county didn't like "Planning and Zoning."

I don't know how we got the zoning district through the legislature the first time. I don't think they fully realized we were taking some of their power away from them. Some of the commissioners were real lulus, serving for 15 and 20 years or more. The legislative body was gerrymandering with districts – which doesn't make any sense – so the people who represent this area met with the commissioners of the various counties.

The legislators were pushed hard enough by the Lee County commissioners and others so when they got back to Tallahassee instead of voting it in, they voted it out. I don't remember how many years this thing went on. When it came back defeated, the reaction on Sanibel was kind of deflated, with citizens feeling like their representatives viewed us as a bunch of hicks over here.

This was in 1960 and what did they do next? Discontent with the county had been building over the past six or eight years. The county knew it would face some serious, organized opposition to its plans for Sanibel.

County commissioners used to represent their own districts, and a long-time commissioner Harry Stringfellow from Pine Island was our commissioner. The main road on Pine Island is named after him, and the only thing that road led to was his house. He pushed to have people elected countywide rather than by district. When the election came, he got 80 or 90 percent of the vote in his district but lost countywide.

Harry Stringfellow from Pine Island was our commissioner.

We thought we were doing something big on Sanibel, something important. At this point, I wasn't opposed to the city, but I still hoped we could accomplish what we needed to do without taking that step. It turned out we couldn't.

SERVING ON CITY COUNCIL

After home rule passed, the Chamber of Commerce, Community Association, Audubon, and other civic groups each appointed two candidates to run for Sanibel City Council. There were 16 candidates! It was a simple election with the top five vote-getters to become the council members.

Bob Taylor was one of the candidates from the Chamber but in the meantime he moved off the island, so the Chamber needed a candidate to replace him. Once again, just like with Mosquito Control, I was in the back of the room at the Community House during the next Chamber meeting, probably half asleep, and they announced "Francis Bailey" to replace Bob Taylor as candidate for city council. I almost fell out of the chair!

It gets complicated from there on out.

The election was so close that a recount was required, and it turned out that I did have more votes. But there was yet another complication to overcome. The law in Florida says you can't hold two elected offices at the same time, and I had previously been elected to the Mosquito Control

I reach out to shake hands with Duane White, who was elected mayor after Vernon MacKenzie resigned.

Board; in fact, I had been serving on that board for 26 years. So I was "unelected" as a city councilman, after which the brand new, first Sanibel City Council appointed me to serve on a temporary basis. I then had to resign my position on the Mosquito Control Board and Sanibel had to hold another election to fill my seat with a permanent council member – and I finally got elected.

It was quite a way to get on the council: elected, unelected, appointed, then another election, all within a few months. I was in and out like a yo-yo. I served 19 years on city council, including a term as mayor. I think that gives me the record!

As you can see, I am wide awake and paying attention, next to Charles LeBuff.

Sanibel's first city council was Porter Goss, who was mayor; Zee Butler; Charles LeBuff; Vernon MacKenzie; and me (I ended up getting the least number of votes).

Zee Butler

I should add a few words here about Zee Butler, because she and I were involved at one time. Zee's first husband Rex was in the Lions Club. I don't know what happened first, either he died or they moved off the island. Zee later married a guy named Butler and then he died and she moved back to Sanibel. At the beginning, we got involved and would go out to dinner together. Then she got cancer. She was first diagnosed with jaundice, and to visit her you had to put on a plastic suit to get into a room with her. Finally an expert came and said she had cancer and the poor woman just went downhill after that. I doubt we would have gotten married. She said I was too indecisive for her.

Back to the city of Sanibel. I was playing golf with Porter Goss – a big Republican – when about halfway through our round a guy came up to Porter and said, "The governor wishes to speak with you." And that was when Porter was appointed to the County Commission. It was Gov. Bob Graham – a big Democrat – and I would love to see Bob become president. The trouble is you can't be very honest and become president, in my opinion. Politicians promise people the moon and give them a street light. I know several people talked about Porter being president. I said, "Forget it. The man's too honest. He can't be president."

I had thought about running for city council and decided against it. Why didn't I want to? You suddenly have a different life, and you can make enemies if you aren't careful. Not that you shouldn't do things that should be done just because you could make enemies. That's not a way to live. Also,

Members of the first Sanibel City Council: me, Charles LeBuff, and our first mayor, Porter Goss.

I had to back off running the store a little bit while I served on council and the store was a big part of my life. Not too long after that, I discovered my store manager was crooked. Maybe if I had been at the store more often that wouldn't have happened.

On that first Sanibel City Council, we arbitrarily drew straws, or the equivalent thereof, to determine who would have the three-year terms and who would have the two-year terms to start with, so the elections of councillors would be staggered. Three councilors took three-year terms, and two took two-year terms. I got one of the two-year terms. Up until the late 1980s or early 1990s, you ran for a seat. Now you just run and a simple plurality wins and you're on the council.

During my tenure, we prepared a time capsule.

At one time we had three council members living in The Dunes a stone's throw from each other: Bob Janes, Bob Davison, and me. It wasn't by ward like most cities.

The years I served on city council were tough years. I'd had enough and I took a three-year break. Then there was a vacancy, and council can appoint someone to fill a vacancy. There was a guy who had registered to run for the seat and he was unopposed; a bunch of people didn't want him to get on council (he later became a councilman anyway). They talked me into running again, and that was the first time I had a real campaign where you spend money. Before that the most I spent was $1.20. They wanted me to run for another term after that and I said, "No, I told you, one year."

In city council they liked to accuse me of sleeping, but I told them I never failed to wake up for the vote. I was always paying attention and always voted to the best of my ability according to what I thought was best for Sanibel. But I didn't mind them teasing me.

After my arm got twisted so many times I thought it would break, I acquiesced to serve a term as mayor. The year I served as mayor was not much different than any other year. If you're

I've been told this cake to congratulate me on my service on council came from Jerry's Supermarket, but I don't believe it.

in charge of a meeting, you can guide it to a certain degree if it's not too controversial. But other than that, the mayor here is only ceremonial. Recent mayors have taken on more work and responsibility. Otherwise, they go to ribbon cuttings and things like that representing the city in addition to the work they do as a city council member.

'My name is Francis, not your honor,' says new mayor

By Don Whitehead

Francis Bailey, one of Sanibel's best known native sons, was elected mayor on Tuesday by the city council in a unanimous vote.

Bailey immediately told his fellow council members "my name is Francis and I don't want any of the 'your Honor' or 'Mister Mayor' stuff." That didn't prevent some councilmen from addressing Bailey as "your Honor" for the remainder of the session.

Bailey took over the gavel from Councilman Duane White, who had been elected mayor one year ago. White stated earlier that he did not want to be a candidate for a second term in the position.

Following Bailey's election, Councilman Charles LeBuff was unanimously named vice-mayor.

The election of Bailey came after Butler withdrew her name from consideration.

hours ago I didn't expect to be mayor. I was boxed in."

In nominating Bailey, Goss stressed that in his view the responsibilities of the job would be less onerous than in the past, and that it was within the spirit of the city charter to rotate the position.

Referring to the arrival this week of City Manager Bernard Murphy, Goss said that he believed there would now be a difference in the role of mayor. He outlined the functions of the job as chairing council meetings, ceremonial, and working with the governor in the event of civil disorder.

With the presence of a new city manager and an established professional team in city hall, said Goss, it is now possible to fully separate the city council from administrative matters, implying that this should include moving council offices out of city hall, and thus making the job of mayor

● continued on A-5

The *Island Reporter* newspaper played a big role in the city's formation. It was founded by Porter Goss and Don Whitehead and Fred Valtin, Duane White and Edwin Underhill. They started it in 1973 when the question of home rule was in its early stages. A couple of times I helped them get the paper ready for mailing but that was about the extent of my involvement.

The Islander newspaper — not the one we know today — pre-dates *The Island Reporter* and some of the people on council didn't go along with its editorial policy — it simply was not sympathetic to the aims and goals of the city council. That paper is not the same one as *The Islander* of today.

I'm not a big supporter of *The Island Reporter* today because they charged 75 cents for it until 2012 when they merged it with *The Islander*. There are too many papers on this island for our size and population anyway. About 10 years ago, maybe longer, I had a reporter come up to me, don't know what paper, who wanted to know what my New Year's resolutions were. I told her I don't make New Year's resolutions, but then when she started out the door, I said, "I'll give you one. We have six publications on this island. We should abolish them all and keep only one, and I don't care which one it is." She walked off in a huff.

Still, if you aren't advertising in those newspapers, it doesn't look good to the community. They have every right to print all these papers, there's free enterprise in this country, but it's ridiculous to have a small community like this with all these papers.

Today I'm a big advocate of the *Island Sun*. I don't know how they print the volume of material they do every week. They have regular columns along with the rest of it. I check the sports statistics, although I think they are ridiculous now – like who has the most strikeouts of all right-handed freckle-faced pitchers on a Sunday afternoon at 2 p.m. with the sun shining, and that's a record.

Sometimes during that period of time we were forming the city, the council members would meet six days a week, occasionally until midnight. We never met on Sunday. It took a lot of time and work. I was not one of the heavy hitters, though, and I didn't do as much as some of the other people. There's no use in my trying to take credit for something I didn't do.

I remember Jean (Nicols) Woodring, Ralph's wife, was the city's first employee, answering phones and such, until she moved up to the planning department when things became a little more sophisticated.

Ralph Woodring's wife, Jean (Nicols) Woodring, was the city's first employee.

Porter and I were never in 100 percent agreement. He thought there was too much commercially zoned land on the island and that it might take a lot of acreage. But back then we disagreed with what someone said, not with who they were. The animosity today and in the last 10 to15 years all over this country is awful – including the Sanibel city government sometimes. Now they get nasty. I can't see that. It's like the guy out west said when you talk about manners: "Miss Post, out here you're not a post at all, you're only a twig."

If I had my druthers, I wouldn't want any chain retail stores on Sanibel. McDonald's wanted to go on the corner of Periwinkle and Tarpon Bay because there was so much traffic. In a way it might have been an asset; there are always two sides to any story. To a degree there are places on the island now that some could see as chain retail or somewhat like it — Cheeburger Cheeburger and some of the clothing stores. Then there's the business about the "cookie cutter" way chains are designed so no matter whether you are in the store in San Francisco, Boston or Sanibel, you can't tell where you are, they all look the same. But not everybody is rich and if you want to take a vacation with your children — I know, I have five — you may have seven meals, and that puts a dent in your pocketbook right off the bat.

Gary Price, our former city manager, said the population including day visitors reaches 32,000 in the winter; I thought that was at least 10,000 too high at the time.

But we fill up those hotels and the condos that really operate like hotels, the ones that rent short-term on the beach, plus the ones that have a one-month limit. It's hard to have an absolute count – some are definite homes, though, and people never rent them. Then there are timeshares. I've always been a little leery of the timeshare thing. It sounds good but then all of a sudden you're assessed for something that you had absolutely nothing to do with. Rules and regulations are set up by the state and some by the condo association.

That 30-day minimum rental requirement always bothered me. I have seen it happen over and over. People first come here for one week, then two weeks, then longer. Then all of a sudden, they're residents. Well, everybody doesn't have enough money to do that. So if you can't rent a place, you're forbidden to come here? I don't think that's right. We have to share our beautiful island.

We set up the Sanibel Plan so as not to have the concentration of people like they do on Fort Myers Beach. But we have people here I call "IGMs"— "I Got Mine" — and they don't want anybody else to come here. Each subsequent person who comes, no matter what the island looks like at the time they happen to get here, says, "The plan is spoiled." But I always say, if you live with evolution

> **...if you live with evolution rather than revolution, you can absorb change.**

rather than revolution, you can absorb change. It's the same way with planning and building. If you build slowly, one house at a time, versus putting up a huge housing development all of a sudden, the neighbors can handle it. There's only so much land and there's only so much waterfront, and we don't want to destroy it so our descendants won't have the same pleasure and enjoyment we have had.

Even though the last year I served on city council was 1994, I still refer to council in the first person, as in "we" did this and "we" did that. It gets in your blood, just like this island does. Leaving council was like most other things: I miss it to a degree but in another way, I was relieved when my last term was over. I felt the same way about being Lion's Club president, a position you hold for one year. The duties take you away from your business and home life, you travel all over the place. After I got through with my year, I felt ready for another year because by then I had learned the ropes. But on the other hand I was glad to get out. What do they call that, a love/hate relationship?

It's hard work serving on council. My softball friend from Fort Myers, Chris Stafford, ran for county commissioner and was elected. He resigned after two years and said, "I didn't know you had to work so hard."

Serving on council is a heavy responsibility, and your decisions affect people's lives. One of the things I was involved in during my time on city council that I felt horrible about was when a widow had built a house with a staircase that encroached, or went beyond the allowable property line. This is a relatively minor thing, but when you're starting up with a land development code in a city like Sanibel, you have to be tough. The rest of the group voted that she had to move the staircase and so did I, and to this day I feel bad. I don't even know who she is. It's funny how things like that stay with you.

Another thing I felt very bad about was the 3-2 vote for the leash law. I was one of the two against that law. I just hated to see that pass. Why should a boy or girl not be allowed to play on the beach with their dog? They have to be chained on a leash? I never walked a dog in my life until the two I have now. When I grew up, we lived with the screen door unlatched and the dogs pushed their way through and came and went as they wanted to.

My wife June's two little dogs, Mei Li and Sin Tu

Every once in a while, the issue comes up of whether city council members should be paid. I have mulled that over in the past. Way back when we were having so much trouble with the county commissioners – they were bums, have I said that already? – you wouldn't really have to have any qualifications to run.

Like any position, if you don't have the means and have to work plus volunteer your time, you can't do it. You have to feed your family. I was fortunate enough to be able to run my business through managers and be able to stay on council. I investigated once while I was on council the question of whether councilors should be paid, to get some younger people. Older people are great, but so are younger people. They have fresh ideas and vinegar; older people have experience and stability.

The Mosquito Control Board had no set salary but we got a stipend for attending a meeting and mileage, stuff like that. One time Wayne Miller, the director of the board, was on the post office steps and somebody was complaining, "How come no one don't ever run for Mosquito Control?" Wayne told him they get $25 a meeting, and the guy answered, "Well no wonder don't no one ever run."

Sanibel City Council was a different story when I was on it. It's getting too damn personal these days. You're supposed to be able to live by Voltaire's rule: "I disagree with what you say but will defend to the death your right to say it." I didn't agree with everybody; sometimes I was kind of a maverick. Porter and I used to butt heads, including as I said about the amount of commercial property that was available. He said there was too much and I said not enough. If you had all the commercial property together in the same place, yes, I would agree, but it's all spread out. But our disagreement didn't mean I had any less respect for him or he for me, I hope.

Porter appointed me to the Centennial Celebration of Lee County and then referred to me jokingly as his "former friend" because of the work that was involved in that celebration.

When you think about it, everything I voted on could have suggested a conflict of interest – because this is my home and my vote affected me and it affected my business. Diversity of views and backgrounds on city council and the planning commission is good.

Ultimately, it all goes back to dollars. There are three ways people can have money: inherit it, earn it, or steal it. With some people it's very obvious they didn't earn it but were born with a silver spoon, or stole it. Look for the responsible people. Some people don't want to balance facts when they face issues on city council or the commission. They just want their way.

The big difference in the council today from my day is the niceties, or the lack of them. Some qualified people – they're retirees – are not used to people saying no to them, no matter what. They may have been successful business people or whatever. They're not used to defeat. If they run and aren't elected, they're horrified. They forget the story of Lincoln, who lost eight elections, failed in two businesses, and suffered a nervous breakdown before he became president.

> **There are three ways people can have money: inherit it, earn it, or steal it.**

I don't like some of the new stuff that's happening on the island, like people building these monstrous multi-million dollar houses — that's fine if they want that, but they don't live in them but a few days a year. They're not part of the community, they don't participate in any way in the community or go to the churches. Even if they stayed six months it might be better. Of course there are a lot of part-timers who do participate, and by the same token there are some full-timers, and even were some back in my earlier days, who do not participate. You can never make a blanket statement, but in general, I think you get my point.

Also, sometimes those huge houses just don't fit in. That's just my opinion. It used to be if you built a house, everybody went to watch it being built. It was an event. Not anymore. It's amazing to me that there's still a lot of building taking place on the island and a lot of buildable vacant lots.

I volunteer as a member and past-president of the local Lions chapter. We're a sociable club but we've also got a purpose. Our main causes are eyesight and diabetes. Also the International Foundation comes to people's rescue in disasters such as the recent earthquake, tsunami, and Hurricane Katrina.

I didn't really choose Lions; there weren't any other groups on the island at the time. I'm the only charter member left. All the civic groups on the island are very friendly. There may be some individuals who are competitive, but some of my best friends are in the other groups.

When we were first in the Lions, you were expected to work, especially if you were an officer. Now some of them go away for six months. I don't think that's right. Everybody's entitled to a vacation, of course, or if it's your wedding anniversary, you'd better be home. But other than that, you should be there.

I started collecting Lions pins because it's fun, that's why I got started. In recent years, it's almost gotten out of hand, the different pins they have. In 1982 or '83 the International Convention was held in Hawaii and a group of Sanibel Lions went out there. My friend Len Yawkee was a big collector and he got me into it, and I've been doing it ever since. I have been to more than 20 national conventions, which is where you have the best chance of picking up pins. I missed a couple because one year June was sick, another year I didn't go to the convention in Taiwan. There are pins for the International Convention, and for state conventions, for the people running for office, collector pins, and pins for foreign countries. I try to stick to U.S. and Canadian pins. If one is particularly attractive to me, though, I'll get it. I've traded pins with people because I could see I was helping them out, giving them a pin they needed for their collection. Recently the families of several Lions who have died gave me their collections. I have thousands of pins.

I LOSE MY BROTHERS

John at the opening of the restored Old Bailey's Store at the Sanibel Historical Museum and Village

John died in 2000, Sam said from taking too many pills, and is buried up in Jacksonville in Mandarin. His funeral was an odd affair, with mules and a procession and both Confederate and American flags draping his plain pine coffin, custom-made overnight by a ranch boarder and John's son Clark.

Sam got sick in 2010, and I thought at first he was going to get well because he came through the brain operation, but in the next couple of days he developed a blood clot. They operated again but that didn't go too well, and it was all downhill from there. It was a benign brain tumor. Sam decided he'd had enough of tubes, yet he wasn't fully conscious. He could squeeze your hand. I was there when we took him home to his house and made him a little more comfortable – no more tubes. The Hope Hospice people had somebody in there around the clock. Apparently Sam was understanding what we said. The next time I came back he wasn't even squeezing hands. I would have stayed up there, but with the condition I'm in myself, I would have been more of a burden than a help.

After Sam died in August 2010, his body was cremated and there was a memorial service in Tampa on a Saturday at the church. For some reason Sam went to a Methodist church, although we were raised Episcopal. There were a lot of football players there. We had a small service for the immediate family, just blood relatives and Cookie. We went down to the beach and his girls said a few things and threw his ashes in the gulf. I've heard Tee said that Sam was the best father in the world. There was a big service for the Sanibel community behind the old school at the Sanibel Historical Museum and Village, which Sam was so instrumental in developing. It was a packed house. When it was my turn to speak, I joked that, "At last, I get to say something," because Sam had so loved speaking in public. I told everyone that Sam could be ornery and grouchy and stubborn but that he was my brother, and I loved him. And that was the truth. I miss him every day, just as I do John.

There was a big service for Sam at which I joked that I would finally get to speak.

SELLING THE HOMESTEAD

Under no condition did I want to get rid of the family homestead; even knowing it was the only thing I could do, it sickened me to have to sell it. In some ways, I feel as though I never moved out. But I came to the conclusion there was just no way I could live there again and no way I could continue to pay the staggering upkeep, taxes and insurance. A lot of work needed to be done to that building. It had been neglected for years.

The heat was never good. And when I pass away, I have so many children and grandchildren, in-laws and outlaws, to divvy it up would be a mess. I have a bunch of bills to pay, too. And did I say lots of grandchildren?

I know there are people who think the Baileys are rich, whatever that means. I have been well-to-do now and then. I can't say I have ever been rich. Right now I'm poor. We did own a lot of land. The trouble with owning land is holding onto it. It's like holding onto the

homestead – it was a small fortune just paying the taxes. I had to keep digging just to find it. I suppose it depends on how you define "rich" and "poor," but land is an awful financial drain, as it was a drain on Daddy. But that particular piece of property, our homestead, is dear to my heart.

The way Daddy got a lot of the land in the first place was that people owed him a lot of money and when there was a hurricane, or during the Depression, or if things just went bust for them, they said, "Here, take my land" in payment of their debt to my father. Land on Sanibel back then was in many ways worth just a little less than zero. Taxes on 40 acres were 43 cents. Back in the 1950s when we started our Mosquito Control District here, the entire assessed value of Sanibel and Captiva was about $10 million. There are houses here today worth more than that.

In Florida during the mid-1920s boom, people would wait until the tide went out and then sell you a lot of useless land. That's a little bit of an exaggerated way to illustrate that some of the dealings were not of the highest ethical quality. Some things are going on now that are reminiscent of those days. Daddy bought property too, but I don't know how he got his property on the gulf. He deeded it to my mother in 1935 so he wouldn't lose it. Those lots used to sell by the front foot, not the square inch, and the price didn't change by the depth. The cost was $5 to $15 a front foot. Priscilla Murphy wanted Daddy to raise the price to $20 and he wouldn't let her. He said, "You're cheating the public."

I'll tell you one way I might have gotten a little closer to being "rich." After Daddy passed away, a lawyer in town, Dixie Beggs, who had been Daddy's lawyer, owned a strip of land west of Rabbit Road and about 150 to 175 feet wide running from the gulf to Sanibel-Captiva Road. He wanted to sell it to me for about $27 per frontage foot. I said to him, "Dixie, that land's not worth that and it never will be." I really had a lot of foresight, didn't I?

Why didn't I buy up all the land? I didn't have the money for one thing, and it was considered worthless at the time. We were considered crazy people living on an island that everyone saw as a mosquito-infested hell hole. During the boom that built Cape Coral and Lehigh Acres and Port Charlotte and other towns around the state, buying land was "a dollar down and a dollar when I can catch you." Sellers had kiosks in Washington DC, Virginia and New York City to sell land in Florida. They wanted people to build but a lot of people wouldn't build in a place where there were no people for miles around. They needed people to attract people.

So, as it has often happened with land in the Bailey family, the homestead became a financial drain, and not a little one. I made up my mind

Rabbit Road land I deemed worthless; a very bad decision.

Sadly, the homestead became a huge financial drain that I couldn't support.

finally after heart-rending contemplation that I just had to sell it. There was no way I was ever going to move back into it with my wife, June, and I had no thought of getting rid of her! The insurance was expensive; the taxes were expensive. At first I worried that my only option was to sell it to a developer – I had to do something with it. But you know how I define a developer? A developer chops down all the trees, brings in a bunch of white sand, brings in a bunch of withered crotons, then sits back and says, "Look at all that beautiful landscaping."

Some time ago I thought about dividing ownership of the homestead without touching the house, but exactly how we could do that equitably among the children was problematic. Anne and Jane were interested, then Jane lost interest so I put it on the back burner. I came up with different ideas, but everything I was considering was leaving the house intact and under my control. And I came to the conclusion that

179

upon my "graduation" from this life, the homestead could cause problems; I decided I needed to do something differently. That said, the homestead represented a big part of my estate. When you have eight children to consider – I have five children and my wife June has three –what you leave behind is important. Then the opportunity arose to sell the house and land to the Sanibel-Captiva Conservation Foundation.

I knew I absolutely could not stand to see a bulldozer going in there as I drove by on my way to work one morning; I just couldn't stand it. But if our family homestead, so dear to all of us, was destroyed by a fire, something natural, maybe I could live with that. It would sort of feel like a cremation. That's when I called the Sanibel Fire Chief Danny Duncan. I said to him, "Would you like to burn that house down as practice for the fire fighters?" Danny said they'd love to but couldn't because the state wouldn't allow it. It was about that time that Tom Uhler, who worked with Erick Lindblad, executive director of the Sanibel-Captiva Conservation Foundation, came up to me and it started to look pretty good that SCCF would buy the homestead and the land on which it sits, which pleased me immensely.

The homestead's facade changed a lot over time.

When I made up my mind to do something with the house, first I had to find out what my brother Sam had to say about it (after all, he was born in that house). Although I had long ago bought out his interest in the house, it is a huge part of our family history and he had a vote as far as I was concerned. I wanted to move it to the Sanibel Historical Museum and Village but Sam didn't want that. I was so surprised, I was just speechless. I couldn't believe it, because the Historical Village meant so much to Sam. But he wanted the homestead to stay on the original property. He felt the same way about the Sears house Shore Haven on Bird Lane, which was the Elinor Dormer's house. He thought it should stay on the bay if they could find a suitable location. There was a big to-do about that some years ago in City Hall. I talked to Sam many times about moving our homestead to the village but his contention was that there was not enough room there and that the village already had an old Sears house and didn't need another one.

Well, Sam got his wish, and now it suits me better too. Sam was right.

So we worked out a deal with the Sanibel-Captiva Conservation Foundation to buy the land, renovate the homestead, and preserve it all. SCCF is restoring the main portion of

At one time, the house had railing along the edge of the roof, almost like a widow's walk.

the original homestead and a small portion will be devoted to Bailey family history. They might have someone living in one side; the details have yet to be worked out as I write this book.

The homestead is comprised of 28.3 acres on Periwinkle Way near the intersection of Donax Street. If it were not for the sale to SCCF, 35 homes could have been built on the property where just one has sat for all these years more than 120 years since 1896. Instead it will be given over to conservation. SCCF will do an initial restoration of the home, first to make it safe, and

will take on the ongoing management of the land in perpetuity. (I have to admit I'm not too happy that they cut down all the bamboo. I hated to see it go. Vegetation is historic, too.)

So we have saved the Bailey Homestead from developers, thanks to SCCF and of course to the Sanibel community, which has been so good to our family.

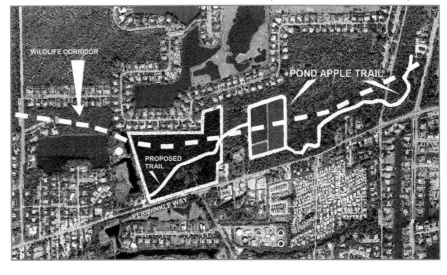

Mankind has been pretty good at developing things but not so good at preserving them. I guess in a few years I won't have to worry about it anymore.

EPILOGUE

Life Today, Mine and Sanibel's

I guess I've slowed down some. I like to say I work as little as I can get away with. I got pretty good at that when I was in the Army. But in reality I go into the store around 9:00 or 9:30 every morning and leave around 5:00, sometimes later, six or seven days a week. I call this "part-time" work. But I fear if I did retire I would never get out of bed in the morning. I have to have something to do. I've thought about volunteering. One of the few regrets I have, if I have any, is that I didn't spend more time at home, for the kids.

In 1999 I got to feeling run down and tired and did something I hadn't done in 20 or 30 years and stayed home from work for two days. I finally went to the doctor when my wife forced me into it. They said I had congestive heart failure – I don't know what the hell that is – and fluid in the lungs. So they drained me out; I still have the holes. They took X-rays, and I felt pretty good. But they said I had a bad aortic valve. That's a critical part of the body, apparently; I was told it needed to be taken care of as soon as I built my strength back up. I also had a little aneurysm. I had to have that taken out, and the surgeons also put in a pig valve.

June didn't like the way I was treated at the hospital in Fort Myers so Steve Brown, a doctor on the island, got me into the Mayo Clinic.

So February 11 was three things: Edison's birthday, my board meeting day in Miami, and my operation. Just before I went into the operating room I talked to the board on speaker phone. June said the next morning after the operation I looked like I was ready to get out and take a race. It worked out wonderfully. I've had so many operations since then I'm like a bionic man.

But I don't know if I could have been so brave as my wife June was when she discovered she had some kind of cancer. After the first time, they said it was all fixed up, but it came back. She went to the Mayo Clinic also. The cancer was contained inside her bladder so they took her whole bladder out and put an appliance in. They asked her, "Right side or left

My wife June is a brave woman.

side?" She stood up, took a golf swing, and said, "Left side." The first thing she wanted to know when she woke up was where her lipstick was. Maybe my operation was the more dangerous one, I don't know, but it was easier to go through than June's.

I've been blessed with a 30-year marriage to June, three wonderful stepchildren in addition to my own children, Anne, Mary Mead, Patrick, Susan and Jane, and Casey Shaw, Linda Stevens, and Bruce Shaw. The year before last on our anniversary, I brought a big bunch of roses home for June and put them on the table. When she got home I kept moving around to lead her in the right direction until she noticed them. She finally did and said, "What are these for, what have you done now?" And I said, "What day is this?" And she said, "Oh! It's our anniversary!" Much later we both realized I was a month early.

John and I after a family Thanksgiving dinner

I have 10 grandchildren to fill the house for holidays and special occasions, and that's more than many other people can say. I especially appreciate it because my Grandmother Bailey died six years before I was born, and because I know how much Granny Matthews meant to me and what a difference she made in my life. I'm lucky too, that I've been able to go to work at a job I love and at a place that means the world to me.

And I saw the green flash one time down in Bimini and I hadn't had a thing to drink! That's worth something. I told you – I've been blessed.

I miss things about the old days, sure I do. But we have to change or we'll just be living in the past. I hate change more than anybody in the world. But we change things at the store, we change at home, we change our underwear.

When Sam came back to the island in the 1980s (he retired his Tampa post in 1979) and became so active and popular while I'd been quietly working at the store and in the community for all those years, it didn't really bother me. We were both doing what we loved.

Sam and I both did what we loved.

**At Islands Night in Hammond Stadium in Fort Myers (left)
and BaileyFest, both traditions started by Sam**

Sam definitely came to the forefront on Sanibel when he came back from Tampa. He had more showman in him than I do, and he loved talking in front of a crowd. He was a much, much better speaker than I am, and he had been doing it for years. Sam started BaileyFest, which has become a wonderful island tradition. The first year we had BaileyFest I wanted to quit it, to be honest; I'm not sure why. There was just something about it; maybe I'm lazy. But Sam pushed it through, there's no ifs, ands, or buts about it. Then there's Islands Night, which is totally, completely Sam's development and a big hit with everyone. He also did a Retail Expo, but that hasn't been nearly as successful.

People used to ask me, "Do you think Sam will come and talk to our group?" I'd answer, "He'll love it. He'll be delighted to help. Your problem will be getting him to stop." Sam didn't make speeches, he talked. If he ran out of facts, he just kept going. For example, he said he had a dog that played left field and my brother John would get so upset and tell him, "You didn't even have a dog!"

John was very opinionated. We were at odds sometimes but when he went away, we started to get along. There were times John and I did a lot together, and other times it would be Sam and me. When John retired from the state Department of Agriculture, Sam used to say John had retired a long time ago and the state just hadn't found out about it.

Clarence Rutland was the same way. He would tell stories about the island and I would say, "Clarence, you know damn well that didn't happen." He'd drawl with a grin on his face, "Well, you got to make a good story."

Clarence and Ruth Rutland

Clarence (I called him Bill Bailey) and Ruth Rutland were our closest neighbors on the island. Apparently when I was born some of the local people wanted me to be named Bill (because of the popular song, Bill Bailey Won't You Please Come Home). Francis is kind of a girlish name – I used to get in fights sometimes to defend my name. Clarence used to call me Bill Bailey, so I called him Bill Bailey, the way kids will do. Miss Ruth worked in the church. Every May Day we used to take flowers down to Miss Ruth. That was before the Russians came along and changed the meaning of May Day to something else. She had a niece who would sometimes come over and play with us.

Clarence was a farmer to a degree and he had a job dragging a thing behind his truck to keep the road smooth. He had been an assistant lighthouse keeper at one time. I never heard him say one bad thing about anybody. But he sure told tall tales!

I always tell people, "If you want a good story, talk to Sam. If you want the truth, talk to me." I'm just another citizen on the island trying to do a job. A lot of our qualities, Sam's and mine, although they're different, I attribute to my father.

When Hodges University invited Sam and me over there in August 2010, we wondered what they wanted. They said, "Don't worry, you're not here for us to reach into your pockets." What they wanted was to give Sam and me an award for having a positive effect on society and serving as examples of good character, essentially. Both of us had the same immediate reaction. We told them, "You've got the wrong people – it should be our father." I don't feel I deserved

At Hodges University with my son-in-law Richard Johnson, granddaughter Bailie, daughter Mary Mead, and John's widow Sally

that award, and at the time I just hoped I didn't have to make any speeches.

If Sam were here, I'm sure he would have made a speech. He was a great storyteller. How much of his stories were true is another question. He loves to tell this one story about playing center field, and there's an alligator somewhere in that story – that is pure unadulterated fiction. But it's a good story. And I miss him. We lost John years ago, and I'm still missing him. They're gone and I can't talk to them about a bunch of silly things we used to do. Every day I come across something I want to ask Sam. When we were kids we tried to have a vegetable stand one time but we sold almost nothing. For the rest of our lives, we used to say to each other, "Ain't got no string beans," and the other would answer, "Don't want any damn carrots." It was just a silly thing, a shared memory, that meant something to us but anyone hearing us would think we were crazy.

I do think about what happens when you "graduate" this life, as I like to refer to it. That's muddy water. I definitely believe in God but sometimes I have hesitancy about the afterlife. It's always puzzled me. I used to say when I was a little boy, if you stop and think about infinity you can never reach it. You can get 1/100,000,000th of an inch from it, but you can never get there. What's out there? Where did we all come from? My contention is that science and the Bible are pretty much compatible. The Bible says God created the Earth in seven days – but we don't know how long a day is to God. It doesn't say how He did it, it just says He did it.

I love dessert and birthday parties, especially mine.

I do believe all the various religions should respect each other. This nonsense of taking the Ten Commandments down or the symbols of Judaism or Islam, I don't like it. These vicious Muslim terrorists are not the true Muslims and unfortunately, they brand all Muslims and it's a shame.

If there's a Judgment Day, do I fear it? I haven't exactly been an angel, but I think very few of us have. There are always some things in life we look back on and wish we hadn't done. I haven't done anything vicious. I think as long as you don't harm other people, you're okay.

I'm just going to have to accept what's out there, or up there – whatever it is that's upstairs or downstairs. One thing I do know – if I get to see just one person in the afterlife, it would be my mother. Being barely 14 when she passed was quite a blow.

Being the last Bailey brother alive is lonely sometimes. I've lost others in my life but there was always somebody to turn to. Now with Sam gone, I think of silly things we used to do, even from 60 years ago. We'd pull our hats down low over our brows and say, "How you?" There were so many childish things between brothers that we continued through our lives. The advantage of being the last brother alive, however, is that I can say a lot of things now and nobody can contradict me!

In one way I would like to be buried in Hollywood Cemetery because that's where my paternal grandfather is, mother and father, two uncles, my aunt, and other relatives. But then on the maternal side they're buried in Kentucky and Fort Myers. Right now I'm thinking of being cremated and spread over the homestead.

To some people the idea of destroying the body is offensive. I've said all my life as far as I'm concerned they can feed me to the buzzards. That's nature. Now I would never do that to anybody else. I would like to explore natural burial, which doesn't harm the earth.

I get upset even now that my father's coffin looked like a female boudoir, with satin and fluff and whatnot – it was ridiculous. I never looked at Mother and Father at their funerals. I refused to go to Mother's. Flossie Hill stayed with us in the Franklin Arms hotel.

When Daddy died, Sam Matthews, my cousin, was the only one who looked at father. Our family doesn't believe in the open caskets. They doctor them all up and leave people with that memory. I don't want to be remembered that way. How do I want to be remembered? Forgotten; that's how I want to be remembered.

SANIBEL'S FUTURE

What I would like to see for Sanibel's future is more people spending more time here. What defines the island has changed over my lifetime. Before the bridge came, I would say it was its isolation. I used to say what Sanibel offered people was this: nothing. A busy lawyer or harried doctor could come here and get away from everything. There was tranquility here.

Fishing on the wooden bridge to Captiva

Of course, that's not true today. Sanibel has lost a lot of its appeal, there's no doubt about it. The people who are starting to come here now are sometimes a different breed of cat. Not everybody.

A lot of contributors here are not residents of the island but call themselves residents – they come back for five, 10, 20 years. They don't live here and are not registered voters but they are very interested in the island. That type of person isn't coming here as much.

Sanibel has lost a lot of its appeal since the causeway brought so much development.

A quiet, isolated road.

More people spending more time here does mean more business for the store but that's not the real reason it's what I would like to see. To keep Sanibel as a community and a friendly place, that's what I care about. Too many people come here and build multi-million dollar houses and don't know Francis Bailey, or any islander, from Adam's off ox. People living in very big houses tend never to make contact with anybody. This is not always true of course. A lot of rich people are the best of citizens. I am being a little harsh here and I'm not talking about everybody. I just think people come and go too much; they live behind gated communities – I hate those things. Gated? Not too many years ago I never even took the keys out of the ignition of the car.

Not everybody who comes here likes it. For example, a Dr. Fairchild who knew Daddy slightly came here with shorts on and the mosquitoes were so thick Daddy suggested long pants. Dr. Fairchild just sort of fluffed off the suggestion – the mosquitoes didn't bother him; other things were more important to him, like the beauty of the island. Some people complained bitterly about the mosquitoes before Mosquito Control. For example, a couple came looking for pond apples – they were very interested in the island's flora – and ended up bitten nearly beyond recognition. Daddy said to them afterwards, "Yes, there are mosquitoes but we just overlook them." While Daddy was never ugly with anybody – he was very quiet – he would simply say, "There's a ferry leaving every hour." I guess now people who feel that way can leave whenever they want.

For some cockeyed reason, there was a time I thought I would want to move to San Diego. Now having been there, that desire has waned. If I had to move somewhere it would probably be Virginia, having spent some time there and having family history there.

But without a doubt, there is nowhere else I would have rather grown up and lived my life than Sanibel.

ONE FINAL NOTE

For the last time, San·i·bel is pronounced:

Săn'ə-bəl)

That's SAN'- ih (barely pronounce this "ih" sound) – bull.

(Source: *The Pronunciation Gazetteer*)

END

84022341R00105

Made in the USA
Lexington, KY
19 March 2018